The DNA of Gutsy Leaders

I'M MADE FOR THIS MOMENT!

Coach Terence H. Biggs II & Dr. Sharon M. Biggs

ISBN 978-0-69234-924-3

DEDICATION

This book is dedicated to all of our fellow leaders who at one time or another had the guts to lead despite any odds, consequences, challenges or outcomes. *I'm made for this moment* doesn't mean major challenges won't surface.

We started this book project in November of 2013 and set out to complete the project by November of 2014. Then, the first obstacle happened: my wife Sharon's breast cancer diagnosis. As gutsy leaders, we were fully engaged in multiple projects which immediately had to be put on hold.

We approached this new *challenge* together by researching and speaking with a team of medical experts (we were collecting data by asking tough questions). After gathering the data, we analyzed our options, prayed and discussed the different treatment options with our medical team. We eliminated all of the *noise* and decided along with our medical team that surgery, radiation therapy, and hormone therapy were the best treatment options for Sharon's early-detected breast cancer.

I am so very proud of how my wife stood toe-to-toe with the enemy of her dreams and aspirations, and she refused to hit the canvas. In addition, in the midst of the diagnosis Sharon continued writing and even published four books! *She was made for that moment* and as a result, I am happy to report that Sharon is cancer-free and healthier than ever!

This would not be the only attempt to derail our DNA book project. As soon as we'd regrouped from the cancer attack, I began having severe spinal issues. An MRI revealed three herniated discs in my neck, which were pressing up against a nerve. The pressure on the nerve caused a level of pain that had me sitting in my pain specialist's waiting area crying like a baby. If I moved or stayed still the pain was excruciating. I recall telling someone who'd asked me to rate the pain on a scale from 1 to 10 that *"My pain has pain!"*

I'm currently being treated for this latest delay, but one thing I know for sure, *I am made for this moment*, and one way or another we will complete this book project, release it to accomplish its mission, and move on to the next project awaiting us. That's just what gutsy leaders do.

Coach Terence H. Biggs II
July 2015

CONTENTS

The DNA of Gutsy Leaders

ACKNOWLEDGMENTS

Sincere thanks to the powerful leaders who believed in and supported this book project enough to give us time from their incredibly loaded schedules to share their personal narratives. Thanks also to Miriam Libove, M.A. and to everyone else who helped edit, proofread and give feedback about the manuscript. We're grateful for your support and encouragement.

INTRODUCTION

As the authors of *The DNA of Gutsy Leaders: I'm Made For This Moment!* we experienced leadership epiphanies when we read Dr. Spencer Johnson's book about the change theory. We found ourselves reading the book (*Who Moved My Cheese?*) several times a year, each time getting new revelations about how to embrace our own radically different leadership skill sets.

We took notes about our personal leadership styles and the styles of others who seemed to disturb the universal status quo during their leadership assignments. Our notes morphed into conversations about writing a simple to read and easy to understand book about *gutsy transformational and situational leaders* who tackle giant leadership moments they seem to be made for.

Our decision was to include narratives from live interviews with leaders who repeatedly demonstrate a gutsy kind of hardwiring to lead. The idea was to write a book that would be *less technical and more practical for leadership development* among practicing and aspiring leaders.

We want our readers to reflect about things like: How do leaders know when it is their moment to lead? How do leaders know what to do and when to do it? What do gutsy leaders seem to have in common with each other?

Pre-Interview Phase

During the preparations we recognized we'd need to develop a set of ten pre-determined questions to ask every leader. Each person got the questions ahead of time to help ignite their thinking before the actual conversations. We did that to avoid having the questions sound like an interrogation. We also wanted to make sure we captured the most authentic parts of everyone's thought process about his or her gutsy leadership journey. As a result, every conversation flowed seamlessly.

The leaders told us the questions forced them to think about who they are as leaders. Interestingly, they also said that prior to their interviews they'd never considered themselves as being gutsy.

Here are the ten questions we asked:

1. What does the term "gutsy transformational leader" mean to you?
2. How did you know when it was your moment to be a gutsy transformational leader?
3. How do you know what to do throughout your evolving gutsy leadership journey?
4. What challenges have you faced as a gutsy transformational leader, and what comes easy to you?
5. Change can anesthetize people. How do you deal with change as a leader?
6. Fear can also anesthetize people. How do you deal with your own fears when you are leading others beyond their fears?

7. If we could use a microscope to examine the DNA of a gutsy transformational leader, what attributes do you believe we would uncover?

8. Describe what goes on viscerally in your body and mentally in your psyche when you are at the peak of a giant moment that demands gutsy leadership.

9. It's been said that there is a leadership vacuum in our nation. As someone who is regarded as a gutsy transformational leader, what advice would you give to up-and-coming leaders?

10. What else do you want us to know about your personal gutsy leadership journey?

Format of Our Book

For months we played around with different formats for the chapters and finally came up with one we believe accurately reflects and preserves the personal narratives.

In the first section, readers get introduced to the leaders based on transcriptions of the conversations with us. The next section talks about common trends that seem to exist among gutsy leaders. Then, we conclude with snippets from our personal leadership stories.

One of our primary goals in writing this book was to create one that is ***brief*** –can be read in a day or two, ***authentic*** –inclusive of actual personal narratives, ***practical*** –useful for book studies and everyday conversations about leadership development, and **versatile** –for the conference table, dinner table, or coffee table.

And, that's the story behind how this small footprint book with a big message about gutsy leadership was developed.

We believe the authenticity of the narratives will help other leaders identify their gutsy leadership DNA and respond to their giant leadership moments.

Coach Terence H. Biggs II and Dr. Sharon M. Biggs
Co-Authors

DNA MOMENTS

"If you know where you're going
you can make the smart choices to get there."
(Pacific Life Insurance TV Commercial)

While watching a *60 Minutes* segment about the October 1993 *Black Hawk Down* event in Somalia, we jotted down some thoughts we believe apply to gutsy leaders.

- Gutsy leaders see and hear where bullets are shot from but they don't sweat or flinch – they continue leading forward to squash the enemy.

- Gutsy leaders view the enemy as nothing more than a deliberate distraction designed to destroy purpose and mission.

- Gutsy leaders can become apologetic when asking for help as if asking for help is a display of weakness versus a demonstration of wisdom.

- Gutsy leaders instinctively take a strategically defensive stance when attacks are hurled at them.

- Gutsy leaders remain clinical yet compassionate in order to keep emotions in check.

- Gutsy leaders take severe and personal hits at very close range and never blame the team.

- Gutsy leaders engage in intense fights that might take all day or all night because they're determined to reach the problem, wrap their minds and arms around the problem, and then lead others to solve the problem.

- Gutsy leaders refuse to leave any wounded behind to die without first trying to rescue them even when the wounded don't know they need rescuing.

- Gutsy leaders can be easily misread by people who misinterpret their clinical compassion as being non-relational detachment and disconnectedness.

- Gutsy leaders stay above deadly political minutiae and keep their ears to the ground so they clearly hear and respond to rumblings.

- Gutsy leaders get thrust into impossible situations and they are wired to produce successful outcomes.

- Gutsy leaders are brave enough to either be on the front line or strategically position others to be on the front line to win battles and conquer the enemy.

- Gutsy leaders are not excuse makers. They dive in, strategize and confront problems.

MEET

THE

LEADERS

Dr. James Caulfield retired in May 2014 after a sixty-year career in Educational Leadership. Dr. Caulfield served for forty-three years in the Union, New Jersey Public Schools and as an adjunct instructor at Seton Hall University (SHU). The Dean and members of the Department of Leadership, Management and Policy asked Dr. Caulfield to investigate and design an accelerated cohort style, fee-based program for practicing K-12 grade school administrators. The program design was aimed at providing the skills and knowledge required of those aspiring to central office positions in New Jersey, throughout the nation, and abroad. For almost twenty years the leadership program has served over five hundred students coming from thirty states and seven foreign lands. Many of the students currently serve as superintendents of schools or in other executive educational leadership positions. Dr. Caulfield served as a Teacher, Counselor, Director of Special Services, Assistant Superintendent, and Superintendent of Schools. He was educated by the Jesuits and served in the U.S. Army during the Korean War. Dr. Caulfield's career of over thirty years of central office service was marked by a number of achievements, culminating in being selected as

Superintendent of the Year for New Jersey; and for a visit by President George H.W. Bush and his wife, Barbara, as well as by several members of the president's cabinet. Dr. Caulfield authored two textbooks on Educational Leadership. During his tenure in Union, New Jersey, he contributed to its successful racial and ethnic integration. He also instituted pre-kindergarten and full-day kindergarten for every child more than twenty years before the models became popular across the country. The Union Public School District was recognized by state and national panels for its students being in the highest ten percent in achievement and for the school district being in the lowest ten percent in cost per pupil. Dr. Caulfield and his wife of sixty years, Regina, live in southern New Jersey. They have three daughters, a son, and nine grandchildren. While at Seton Hall, Dr. and Mrs. Caulfield hosted a reception and dinner for SHU cohort members each summer at their Spring Lake summer home. Dr. Caulfield is driven by his unwavering faith and by his dedication to serve others. In addition to Dr. Caulfield's other accomplishments, he earned a Doctor of Education degree in Administration, a Master of Arts degree in Education, and a Bachelor of Science degree in Mathematics. He serves as President of Caulfield Associates, Inc., a consulting firm established in 1994 that specializes in Resource Management, Cost Containment, Quality Control, Strategic Planning, Computer Instruction and Networking, Distance Learning, Grantsmanship, and Plant Expansion. Dr. Caulfield's executive appointments and consultation initiatives include *Whittle Communications; President Appointment, U.S. Department of Defense; Board of Directors, Wireless Cable Association International; Chairman, Education Committee, Wireless Cable Association, International; U.S. Senate, Committee on Education; Committee on Economic Development; Wireless Cable-Ireland; Wireless Cable International; New Jersey Department of Education; New Jersey Department of Higher Education.*

Terence H. Biggs II, Dr. Sharon M. Biggs and Dr. James Caulfield are pictured above. This "selfie" was taken on Sunday, February 9, 2014 in Dr. Caulfield's Seton Hall University office immediately following his book interview. Dr. Caulfield interviewed Dr. Biggs in 2011 for her membership in Cohort XV of SHU's Two-Year Executive Educational Leadership Doctoral Program. In 2012 the cohort celebrated Dr. Caulfield's 85th birthday with him.

Dr. James Caulfield
The Meaning of Gutsy Leadership

My first thought about the word gutsy is that I don't like the word. I would say proactive rather than gutsy. Gutsy didn't resonate with me very well. I'm just sharing my opinion.

We Say What Others Are Afraid to Say

A large urban district proposed to take over the administration of the student selection process (lottery) for a charter school I helped to establish. A reporter quoted me as saying to their central office administrator, 'You haven't been very successful at what you're doing. Why would you take from us something that has been working? Our students are in the top ten percent in the state in test scores and we spend four or five thousand dollars less than some other urban districts do.' That statement was printed in the paper and the district superintendent wasn't happy. My comments were bold but I believed that someone had to proactively state the truth, so I did just that.

Being Proactive Sets Some Leaders Apart from Others

I have found that some school superintendents I encountered were reactionary people. They seemed happy to be custodial caretakers. I don't know if you ever noticed how firemen operate, but they sit in front of the firehouse with their chairs tilted back against the wall and wait for emergencies. I've found that's what some district superintendents do. They react to district fires instead of staying in the trenches to head things off before they even start. I always chose to be proactive in my leadership and that choice served me well.

I started to notice that other district superintendents watched me and began imitating what I did. For example, when I introduced preschool and full-day kindergarten twenty-five years ago other superintendents did the same thing. I never operated on the basis of simply maintaining the organization because that would have made me a manager versus a leader. As I led it not only helped my district make progress, it helped other districts innovate because their superintendents followed my lead.

Lead from Your Core

I think a transformational leader is somebody who studies an issue in education and does the right thing. The person moves in the right direction not based upon other adults, but upon trying to provide equal opportunities for students. I was Jesuit educated, which remains the fundamental driving force in my life. I've always led the way that I did in order to gain heaven and I believe every student has a soul and is destined for salvation. To me that meant that every child deserved an equal opportunity to attain success.

Be a Bold Pioneer

In the Union Public Schools I introduced dozens of innovations. I was the first district superintendent to institute an ROTC program. At the time it was soon after the Vietnam War and people said I was teaching war so they came out against the program. I rallied enough people who were veterans and who helped us to win that debate so we could offer one hundred kids an alternative path to high
school graduation. The students wouldn't write a composition for their English teachers but they would write one for the Colonel of the ROTC program. Those one hundred students happened to be mostly minority and they often didn't have fathers at home. When they got their report cards they took them to the Colonel or to the Sargent. When they got into trouble the Colonel or the Sargent said to the principal, 'Don't send them to detention. We'll take them on Saturday mornings and put them to work.' The students loved it. As other superintendents saw how much success we were having with this segment of students they started implementing

ROTC programs in their high schools. The driving force for me was to provide an equal opportunity to students who might have otherwise dropped out of school.

Assess Whose Needs You're Meeting

I started teaching sixth grade and I had some students with 80 IQs and some with 160 IQs in the same room. By the end of the first half of my first year of teaching I had lost all of my students' interest because I was driven by the curriculum and never paid attention to their aptitudes or their scholastic ability. By December none of them were raising their hands to participate in class except for one boy. Ed K. was still raising his hand. He transferred out during Christmas Break and then I had nobody left. I had to step back and look and say, 'What can they do?' After my first year I learned that being mission-driven to meet actual needs is one of the most important things to focus on as a leader.

Your DNA Guides You to the Right Position for You

I spent my entire career in the Union, New Jersey school district. I got the job with my uniform on in 1952 and I spent forty-three years there. I never wanted to go anyplace else so I never applied for any other jobs. In those days, you were called by the main office secretary and she'd say, 'Jim, there's a guidance counselor's job. Jim, there's a head of special services job. Jim, there's an assistant superintendent opening.'

The board president called me one day when Regina and I were on the golf course. The board president said, 'Jim, do you want to be superintendent?' I said, 'Well. Okay.' If I had been assistant for life, that would have been alright. Or, if I was a teacher or head of special services for life that would have been okay. But, I said 'Okay, I'll be the superintendent.' It seemed like the right fit for me at that point in my leadership career and it turned out to be a good decision.

Take Action When People Get Disappointed in You

As you continue making progress in your leadership you can expect that eventually people will become disappointed in you for one reason or another. They'll get mad at you over something they believe you're not doing well.

One school board member came to me upset one day and said, 'We don't get enough attention in the newspapers.' I said, 'What do you mean? We're doing all these great things in the district and getting publicity all the time.' The person said, 'No, I am not being mentioned in the papers.' After that conversation I started writing little blurbs about the person and they would read the announcements at the board meetings. Sometimes it was easy to address disappointments with simple fixes like writing blurbs with someone's name in them.

Surround Yourself with Ambitious Folks to Help Seize Your Leadership Moments

I always liked people who were ambitious and who were using their positions as stepping stones. Those individuals did more to cooperate on innovations because it would look good on their resumes. Those were the same people I relied on to help me push gutsy initiatives along because they were always up for the challenge.

I always knew when it was my moment to lead because the Jesuits taught you to lead and serve others. My training was not to be a status quo leader, but to see what had to be done and to do it. At meetings for school administrators, even at the national level, I always said what I believed. Apparently, people took notice of what I said and did.

People Listen Even When They Dislike You

My superintendent once said to me, 'The other administrators don't understand your vocabulary.' I said, 'What do you mean?' I didn't realize I was saying anything that sounded erudite or pompous because at meetings I just said what I thought. Evidently people paid attention.

The district consisted of administrators who had grown up and worked in Union their whole lives. They expected to be appointed superintendent so I didn't realize that when I became superintendent I immediately became unpopular. I was unpopular but they still listened to my ideas because they were good for the district as a whole.

Try to Learn the Network's Political Fabric and Culture

Being an outsider meant that I had to work hard to learn and understand the political fabric that existed in the community. When I'd go to a township committee meeting the mayor would call out to a friend who was an administrator, 'Hello, Harry. How is your mother?' That kind of political system was in place.

Even after forty-three years I still hadn't defined all of the networks and the relationships among people in the district. For example, the cafeteria manager was the sister of the board president. I learned a lot of the network but I was still surprised when I left because I'd see another network like one of the school nurses being related to someone in maintenance.

Choose Battles Wisely

I took on battles that I had some chance of winning. I realized I would lose on some of the initiatives that I put in place but I just knew what to do. I would weigh the options and the choices and figure the alternatives and make decisions. There were things I did that at the time I knew would be unpopular. For instance, the time that the district lost two thousand students because the birthrate declined in the 1970s was a challenging time that called for wise and tough decisions to be made. The township committee had designated which schools they wanted closed so I said, 'You either close schools and sell them off or rent them to outside groups. Or, you add preschool and full-day kindergarten so we can increase student enrollment.' That idea didn't go over well so I said, 'Without adding any staff.' Of course, I didn't talk about the number of staff I could lose if I shut the schools down.

I added, 'With the status quo we won't spend any more money than we have been spending. If you're not ready for preschool and full-day kindergarten, let's try them as pilot programs. Let's say we run a nine-week program of preschool for four year olds and we set the entry cut-off at December 31st instead of October. I want to get the students early because they're just home watching television or at some nursery school.'

The board listened and thought, *Oh, that's pretty good.* Boards want to know that they're not taking chances and that they have a good likelihood of being re-elected. They want to have the people's support.

So, we ran a nine-week preschool pilot program and it just exploded with interest. I said to myself, 'You know, since they're tolerating preschool they can tolerate full-day kindergarten.' I recommended another pilot program called full-day kindergarten.

Pretty soon the board became suspicious of the term *pilot program* because I introduced so many programs that way. They then passed a board resolution saying that I could not introduce any other programs without their approval. By then we had so many successful programs operating, many of which started out as pilots, and people in the district had begun to believe in my ideas.

Always Act on the Basis of Sound Principle and Virtue

I believe integrity goes a long way and I don't say that with glibness. Some people show themselves to operate based on their own self-interests. The school district never could quite understand that I had no ulterior motive and that everything I did was done based on sound principle and virtue.

For example, when the township needed space for a senior center and I had the space in the district I said, 'How about using the front section of Burnet Junior High? You can pay the district twenty thousand dollars per year and you'll have to agree to renovate. You redo the balcony and we'll put classrooms up there, as well.'

Although they agreed to that arrangement they forever tried to figure out if I had an edge or was up to something other than trying to build an excellent school district and help the community.

My value system guides me to believe that every person is created in the image and likeness of God. I do things because they're the right things to do for people.

Let Integrity Win Over Your Opposition

It became a little more difficult to get support of my ideas when one board member's election turned the once Democratic board into a Republican board. The new board president thought I had coordinated with the Democrats and had given them a roster of teachers who lived in town who would rally against him. One day the board president rushed into my office and said, 'Give me that roster!' I said, 'I have no roster. I gave nothing to anybody.' Within a year that same board president was in my basement watching the Super Bowl with me. He'd begun to realize that I was doing good things for the district and he even said to the rest of the board, 'Why are you fighting Caulfield? He's five years ahead of you. Just, rely on him because he's not making mistakes and he won't take the district down the wrong road.'

Find the Table, Sit Down, and Join the Feast

The board president was a fellow who held meetings in a tavern. Whatever was to happen on the stage in front of the public during the general meetings was discussed. We'd all go down to this barroom and the board president would order pizza and we'd have the *board meeting*. We had dual control at the time with the board, the business administrator and I sharing control. It was workable for decision making. One day I said to the business administrator, 'You'd better start attending the meetings.' He was confused and said, 'I do attend every meeting.' I said, 'No, I mean the *real* meetings.' Leaders have to stay aware of when the meeting before the meeting will take place and then find a way to be in attendance. That's where most of the actual decisions are made. One quote goes like this, 'If you're not at the table you're probably on the menu.' I never wanted to be on any board's menu so I found ways to sit at the meeting table even though my ideology was dramatically different from that of the board president and some others.

Be an Inclusive Leader

We integrated the schools in Union in 1969 when I was the assistant superintendent. The reason we were investigated was because the southern states were angry and said, 'Why don't you investigate states in the north? There's actually a lot of segregation in the north.' The officials picked a bunch of districts to investigate including Union, New Jersey.

Long before my time there were no attendance barriers between the minority neighborhood and the non-minority neighborhood. Attendance areas were later established by board resolution separating the neighborhoods. *We had to integrate.* As the district leader I was determined to establish a school district that was inclusive of *all* of the students who lived in the area.

Strategically Plan

As a district we integrated and I was in charge of the integration plan. The integration plan called for minority students in grade kindergarten through grade five to be transported out of Jefferson School, which was predominantly minority. In the sixth grade all of the non-minority kids would be transported to Jefferson School.

The final plan involved all seven elementary schools. The board of education had acted heroically in the eyes of the public.

Help People Remember Your Legacy

As well thought out as our district integration plan was, there were still some parents who said they'd throw themselves under the school bus before allowing their children to attend integrated schools. I went to every bus stop in the minority neighborhood. I walked in the rain through the neighborhood and at each bus stop helped five year old kindergarteners onto the buses. The minority parents told me they never forgot me doing that even when we'd have our differences about other issues over the years.

See Growth Potential in Every Challenge

District integration was a challenge. Teacher strikes were also challenges. When I was assistant superintendent, the superintendent had to deal with a teacher strike and he couldn't understand why people were picketing when he had been the principal of their school in the past. The superintendent couldn't reconcile that it was okay for teachers to picket because a strike was their way of getting equal treatment.

When I started there was no such thing as a teachers' union and boards treated teachers like serfs. The boards would let us attend board meetings to make salary proposals and before we left the room they would have posted the new salary guide for the upcoming year. Back then boards scoffed, ignored and embarrassed teachers at will. Many of the administrators supported the teachers' union back then because most of them had actually started as union organizers.

Nevertheless, the superintendent left the district soon after the strike. I became superintendent not too long after that. We got injunctions so we did the appropriate things you do as management when there's a strike or a threat of a strike. You didn't do these things because you felt any vindictiveness toward the teachers, it was merely protocol.

Years later when I was superintendent the teachers threatened to go on strike because they said I had not abided by an article in the teachers' contract. When that was announced I put an ad in the *Times* offering two hundred and fifty dollars pay for teachers to temporarily fill positions. Candidates came from Florida and from all over the country to New Jersey and they lined up from my office down to the center of town.

The union president and other teachers from the union stormed my office when they saw all of the hiring stations where we were taking candidates' names and administering timed tests after reviewing their teaching certificates. The teachers' union folks said, 'You must be paranoid, Caulfield.' I said, 'Well. What did you do last night after the meeting that lasted until three in the morning? The meeting that I thought was pretty productive?' I had asked for another twenty dollars on the deductible or something. They left the meeting and created a flyer that said, *Terrible meeting. Caulfield blah, blah, blah. What are you prepared to do?'*

I translated their actions as a strike threat so I immediately placed an ad in the paper. The union representatives said, 'We never intended to strike,' and I told them that based on the flyer it looked as if they'd already gone on strike. They flexed a little more and said, 'If we do go on strike we'll shut down the district!' I agreed with them and told them that they would do just that because they were pros who knew what they were doing. They left seething but there was no strike.

See Excitement in Challenges

The strike when I was assistant superintendent was an exciting time of giving out subpoenas. As superintendent I had two attempts at strikes but they both failed because I don't believe their hearts were in it by then. The superintendent before me who resigned came back to visit when I was superintendent and guess who was in the office next to mine as my assistant? The person who had led the strike when the former superintendent was there!

Add the Right People to Your Team

I worked in a factory and found out that the people who organized the union were oftentimes promoted. They were promoted, one because they were a little more capable, but also it took them right out of the union activities.

That's what I did when I appointed the head of the teachers' union to be my assistant. He became one of my most loyal staff members and he knew the inner workings of the union. He was more militant than I was because he knew exactly which staff members were less motivated and which ones were system gamers. In fact, when somebody requested a personal day that wasn't on the schedule they'd go to him and he'd say, 'Absolutely not. But go ask Caulfield.' That person became one of my best enforcers and he took care of some of the administrative things so that I could visit schools and be a visible presence.

Be Visible and Relational

I went to schools to visit classrooms twice a week on Tuesdays and Thursdays. I would talk with teachers, students, principals, custodians, secretaries, and everyone else in the buildings as I made my way down the halls. I kept a little pad with me and I would always send principals and teachers notes ahead of time to let them know I'd be visiting. Folks would get their hair done and give their best lessons. I didn't want their worst lessons. I wanted their best. I'd write them notes about my visits, which they'd put up on the chalkboard. The simple act of visiting the schools and talking with people helped me build very solid relationships during the forty-three years I was there.

Lead from the Front

I also gave a state of the school system address at each school to keep people informed about what was going on throughout the district. I believed in not only being visible but in being proactive by not sneaking up on people unexpectedly. Keeping people informed allowed me more opportunities to lead them instead of having to manage their behaviors and actions.

Some people will be uncomfortable with this kind of leading from the front. For instance, the principals were sensitized because during my visits I would look around and ask lots of questions about what was going on in the schools. Custodians and elementary school teachers were always more free to talk about what was really going on so I spent a great deal of time visiting with and listening to them. They gave me good information that helped with districtwide decisions that I needed to make.

Stop the In-Fighting Before it Stunts Your Vision

I called the mayor one day and said, 'We're not passing any school budgets so why don't you stop this in-fighting and get along with each other?' All the mayor had to do was put out the word and the budget wouldn't pass. When only ten percent of the people in the community ever voted on the school budget anyway, the mayor had enough people on his staff alone to kill the budget.

The mayor said, 'Okay, Jim.' And then he paused before he said, 'As soon as I wipe them all out,' which he proceeded to do. There were factions that were destroying every opportunity to pass school budgets. Once they were gone the budgets passed and we were able to continue moving district innovations forward.

Build a Legacy That's Tough to Follow

I knew that the person who followed me as superintendent would have a tough time being accepted because of all of the successful programs that I'd implemented. I even said to my assistant superintendent, 'Don't follow me. Let somebody else take it for five years because by then they'll forget about me.' He didn't take my advice.

I remember being in a local diner after I'd left the district and somebody yelled down the entire length, 'Why did you ever leave? When are you coming back?' I'd been successful in garnering support to create an entirely new and improved school system.

Create Organizations and Systems Fit for Dignitaries

It was also exciting when the president came to Union for a visit. The visit came about when I met in Washington with sixteen other district superintendents from across the nation, all of whom had agreed to implement the reforms that the governors' association had written up in the book called *Time for Results*. We'd all volunteered to meet every six months, and every two years the president would either meet in the White House with a superintendent or he'd visit a school district.

The decision was made for the president to visit a district one particular year. I raised my hand right away to volunteer Union to be the visitation site and six months later the FBI and the secret service all descended on Union.

The secret service people were interested in safety and security while the White House staff was interested in exposure and public relations. The secret service came in talking about what they were doing like putting up a canopy over the driveway so that nobody could shoot the president. The White House staff talked about having the students leave the building and surround the asphalt so that they could all shake hands with the president.

Finally it got closer to the visit and at the last minute they told us what the visitation route would be. Secret Service also told people, 'You have to be out of those houses in the area because we see the shadows of the people inside and that could be a security issue.'

One of the White House staff members came to me and said, 'A letter from one of your students got through to the president.' In the district we were actually celebrating the Presidential Fitness Awards and that was one of the occasions for the president's visit to Union. Part of the visit would involve a talk between the president and some of the local superintendents.

The letter that got through to the president said, '*I'm in special education and we try hard, too.*' The students with special needs heard the fitness awards were for students with the highest academic records. The White House staff person said to me, "Where's that child who wrote the letter going to stand? I said, 'In front of Hamilton School, but why would you ask?' The staff member said, 'The president's going to get out of the car and walk over, read the letter and hug the child. Barbara Bush will be right next to him.' I said, 'Have you told the secret service?' The White House staff person said, 'God, no! Aw, no!'

I was the only person who knew this plan outside of the White House staff folks and I knew something bad could happen at any moment. The president's plane landed and we greeted him, got into the cars, and then the entourage headed down the streets through town.

All the secret service people were right there and I held my breath because I was in the second car. I saw the president's car stop and President Bush jumped out and ran over to where the student was standing. He read the letter and walked along shaking hands with all of the kids.

That was an exciting and proud time for the district. I was especially proud when the president said, 'This is one of the greatest school systems and the best superintendent.' We had created a district fit for a dignitary's enjoyment.

Lead Beyond Failures and Power Trips

If you know what you're doing is right and you realize that some budgets might fail even though you kill yourself to get them passed, you can still lead people through change. Some of the things you want to do are just beyond the reach of the board and they'll have to say 'No.' It's important to recognize that board members who are running tend to want to cut budgets by large amounts because they want to show the community their new power.

First year board members are usually staunch supporters of the budget. Instead of fighting them I'd host forums to explain the consequences of a failed budget. I'd share presentation slides about things like guidance counselors needing to be fired, librarians and coaches needing to be fired. No board member wants that to happen under his or her watch.

I knew I would not be able to pass a bond referendum because people didn't want it. I brought in the opposition and said I'd put lights on the field for one hundred and twenty thousand dollars and buy new band uniforms that cost eighty thousand dollars. Having new lights on the field would mean that we could play on Friday nights. The referendum passed two to one all because I paid tribute to those opposing groups.

Play the Game – Win Some, Lose Some

Leaders have to recognize things are not always going to go well for them. You still have to take calculated and well thought out chances that will benefit the groups you're serving. I once knew a superintendent who said his job was to go around and cause trouble. He succeeded at that and didn't last long as a superintendent. Stirring up trouble was never my motive so I was braced to live with the consequences of my district decisions. I went after success but stayed prepared to lose bond referendums and budgets, and to sometimes alienate board members. That didn't stop me from running workshops for the public and for local realtors to keep them informed about what was going on in the district that I worked so hard to move forward.

You Control the Agenda

Another way I kept people informed was to send home a weekly memo about district initiatives. By doing that I was controlling the agenda for priority issues that needed to be addressed. I was doing it for good reason. But, they could see what was gonna be on the agenda. Either *you* control the agenda as the leader or *they* control it. By providing information all the time people can see the framework of what's on the horizon.

I always had the curriculum group, a group of administrators, and the special education teachers at the informational meetings. I was constantly listening to what they had to say. Then I would send out newsletters to them about what was discussed at the meetings. They asked tough questions. At times they complained that I didn't answer their questions, but we always continued having the informational meetings. When I was preparing to leave the district the groups asked, 'What do you want us to do?' I said, 'Name a building after me,' which they did. I said, 'I spent my life here.' I believe that tribute had a lot to do with me keeping everyone informed while I controlled the agenda of what we discussed.

Transform an Organization One System at a Time

I established a Shop Rite Supermarket in the high school in Union. I wanted a fully-functioning supermarket so the special education kids could learn how to stack merchandise and train to become cashiers. The YMCA needed space so I put in a childcare center where children from age six months old could be cared for. There was also a health program for the girls so they could learn about the health industry and then work at the local hospital.

I put a senior day care center in the high school so the students got used to intergenerational relationships and Alzheimer's cases. The kids who went in to the center kept logs on the senior citizens so that when they died they could gift the log diaries to the families.

We used to have Title III and IV competitive grants. I got one to develop science kits and we sold them to McGraw Hill and they marketed them. In the meantime I said to state officials, 'I really need to experiment with these kits before we market them, and I need a television system for the high school.' That was before cable was in place. McGraw Hill actually gave me the money to put up the tower to build a color studio in the high school so we could introduce Communication Arts to another whole group of kids who were not as enchanted with the Latin and Greek being taught in some of the classes.

Then, I got a call from a major television network saying, 'We need your transmitter. We know you're licensed and we can't get those frequencies at our station. Can we borrow your frequencies? We need your transmitter because you have a wireless cable system and we'll give you one hundred thousand dollars a year just to let us use your unused time.' We were obligated to broadcast sixteen hours a week but the network could use our channel the rest of the time to broadcast entertainment programs. From that point on the district received approximately one hundred thousand dollars a year. When wireless services and cell phones came along the same frequencies were sold to private cable companies by the board of education for a seven-figure price.

I put a bank in the high school because the president of the bank said, 'You're not sending me any cashiers.' I felt like saying, 'We're not sending you any cashiers because the students can make more money at McDonald's.' Instead, I said, 'If you put a bank in the high school where my kids will be trained I will introduce a banking curriculum to the students.' The bank is still there servicing one hundred and forty teachers and all the parents and students.

The whole idea was to create a system where the less motivated students would like the program enough to stay in school and graduate with marketable skills.

Try New Things Out with *Pilot* Initiatives to Help People Move Beyond Their Fears

When people in the organization are afraid to make changes I think the first thing leaders need to do is inform them about what's going on and why versus shocking them into dramatic changes. I would always inform groups to give them time to adapt to new things by having pilot programs.

I remember I had a meeting with parents and towns people when I wanted to change the school configuration. One of the board members said to me after the meeting, 'You've already made up your mind, why are you bothering asking?' And, I said, 'Gee. Is it that obvious?' I once talked to the supervisor who introduced the banking program and she said, 'Just tell me what you want. Don't really worry about what I think because I'll do whatever you tell me.'

I think overloading people with information about what you think is good and right and just for the organization will help them overcome any anxiety and fear.

The high school couldn't believe what I was prepared to do next. I was going to *pilot* a fully functioning post office in the high school but I didn't get to do it before I left.

Gutsy DNA Legacy

Your leadership has to be about values and not about self-promotion. My daughter Maryrose is now a superintendent in Rumson, which she loves. The community loves her and I believe she'll follow in her father's footsteps. She's working with teachers and administrators on the new teacher evaluation system and the union representatives thanked her for her efforts with the evaluation system. It's not every day that you hear about a teachers' union thanking a district superintendent for the work he or she does.

Love What You Do and Stand by Your Convictions

You've got to love the job of district superintendent. I never asked about a raise for myself but I did ask for my staff. I believe that if money is not your motive you can accomplish more.

Powerful Leadership Sensations

The best way for me to describe my leadership journey is to say that it was pure excitement. Sitting around waiting for something to happen would not have been exciting. Even the strike was a moment of truth because the board was not interested in paying the teachers more money and I was interested in preserving the contract so I could control what was going on. The board was willing to give anything as long as it didn't show up in the paper as a salary raise. That led to moments of excitement every day.

Integration was another moment of glory even though there were threats to harm the former superintendent and he needed a police escort. I walked every neighborhood and every street and kept kids from different neighborhoods getting on the same buses with each other to go to and from the same schools. They studied together and that allowed us to preserve the neighborhood even though the students were in seven different neighborhood schools. Integration worked. With thirty buses and eighty bus stops someone could have been harmed. No one was.

The achievement of the minority students doubled within one year and by the time I left a greater percentage of minority students were going to college than non-minority students.

Have the Guts to Withstand *Coercive Persuasion*

Leaders just have to do the right thing no matter what's going on around them. It takes the word *gutsy* to withstand the persuasive powers. I guess I do like that word after all.

Closing Thoughts from a Leadership Legend

At eighty-eight years old I'm still leading from my core by consulting with the Robert Treat Academy Charter School, which has a one-hundred percent minority student population. The school's graduates go on to some of the most prestigious private high schools in the country and then to Ivy League colleges and universities.

Thank you. This interview has been a joy. Good luck with this book project. I do want that photo back for my obituary. My daughter who's a judge is the executor. I already sent her my obituary and asked, 'How is it?' She said, 'Pretty good.' She'll have the guts to do something better.

Ms. Judy Chapman Killion of northern New Jersey founded Garden State Woman (GSW) in 1988. Born to blue collar parents with less than high school educations, Judy and her two siblings flourished under the tutelage of hard working, devoted parents. *"My work ethic and moral compass were molded when I was growing up. My father worked three jobs, as a milkman, landscaper and janitor. My mother was basically a stay-at-home mom who did part-time work. Our frugal upbringing was a gift they gave us. We were not allowed to open the refrigerator door without permission. This was because my mother had every meal planned from paycheck to paycheck. The one thing that they never put limits on was our future. We were taught to believe that if we were willing to make the effort and work hard, anything was possible."* Ms. Chapman Killion says that GSW represented the fruition of what she and her family believed. The mission is to encourage women to believe in themselves and to be undaunted in their quests for success and happiness in all aspects of their lives. Ms. Chapman Killion says that this is easier said than done because of cultural limitations that are gender-related and affect women. GSW seeks to be a role-model for successful women by encouraging women to not see themselves as victims, and to regularly access the up-to-date and verifiable information, and the networking opportunities that GSW offers, primarily through its website, www.gswoman.com, e-newsletters, conferences, and networking events. GSW profiles women who are difference makers and role models, with a target audience of women business owners, entrepreneurs, corporate, and professional women. Since 1998 GSW has been an advocate for New Jersey women, and it has been recognized with numerous awards including the 2012 U.S. Small Business Administration Women in Business Champion of the Year. Ms. Chapman Killion was named by the Association for Women in Communications Northern New Jersey Professional Chapter to receive its "Women Who Will Lead, Mentor and Succeed" award. GSW published Annual Financial and Health Guides and hosted high impact financial, health and career conferences. In 2007, the Garden State Woman Education Foundation (GSWEF) was founded as a 501 (c) 3 organization. The foundation provides tuition assistance to inner-city young women who have been accepted into a New Jersey college or university. In 2014, the foundation's programming forged a new collaboration with Rutgers School of Business-Newark and hosted a state-wide event in May of 2014. Inner-city high school students were invited to attend the day-long networking event. Ms. Chapman Killion has plans to expand the program to high schools, colleges and universities throughout New Jersey for the early recruitment of young women who show an interest in pursuing a business education to prepare for college and careers. Ms. Chapman Killion has a Bachelor of Arts degree from Rutgers University and successfully completed the Berkeley School of Secretarial Training in East Orange, New Jersey. Her other career accomplishments include serving as Assistant to the Secretary of British Computer Society in London, England; Assistant to the President, Republic Systems & Software; Director of Public Relations, Mountainside Hospital, Montclair, New Jersey; Director of Development & Public Relations, East Orange New Jersey General Hospital, and Owner of Walnut Farm, Long Valley, New Jersey. She and her husband, Jack Killion, were married in 1961 and have a son, Jonathan, who is a graduate of Delbarton Independent College Preparatory School for Boys and Georgetown University. Ms. Chapman Killion owns two horses, two dogs (a German Shepherd and a Bull Dog) and one parrot, which she raises and cares for on her family's Long Valley, New Jersey thoroughbred breeding and racing farm.

Judy Chapman Killion

Finding Opportunities in Chaos

A gutsy transformational leader is someone who sees opportunity among chaos. I can actually make that thought personal. We have only one child and in raising him my point of view was the one thing you can give your child is an education. When the Mercedes gets recalled they still have their education. I paid a lot of attention to Jonathan's schooling. He did fine but I was frustrated because I didn't believe he was learning. This was a very chaotic time for me and I just kept pounding away until I finally solved the problem to *my* satisfaction by getting him into a school where I felt he was learning.

I think for women in particular you have to rely on those gut feelings. I'm not a feminist in the traditional sense but I'm a feminist based on the fact that I think intellectually gender shouldn't hold you back. Sometimes you need to step outside of your box and pursue what you think is a good thing regardless of how chaotic things around you might be.

Garden State Woman

We raised our son out here in Morris County, which is

a bit of a cocoon in New Jersey. We met a lot of successful women doing great things and we realized many of them had corporate responsibilities not unlike the responsibilities their husbands had. The women might need to be in California on Monday morning for a board meeting and one of the pipes breaks in the house, or one of the kids gets sick.

We realized that the one real thing the women in the community didn't seem to have was enough time to get everything done. It takes time to find good information so the editorial input behind *Garden State Woman* was to provide resources and information to thriving women. We didn't focus on women who saw themselves as victims, but instead the focus was on women who wanted to do things right and well.

During those times we had a print publication. We kept that going for thirteen years. Our advertising support came from the Merrill Lynch's of the world. It was corporate supported because businesses recognized women had their own income and made their own decisions. Once the corporate marketing budgets disappeared our funds dried up.

We had a website all along so we shifted gears and made the website a priority. We also did conferences, which we're still doing. That's just one example of leadership by not throwing in the towel and scrambling around to re-invent yourself. It worked.

Identify and Seize *Your* Moments

For women, some of our leadership moments involve our families. I was one of those wonderful *older* moms who had some discretionary income so I could do things with our son. One of my goals was to travel so Jonathan and I traveled every summer and Jack would stay home and make sure the credit card bills were paid. I wanted to drive Jonathan to every one of the fifty states in our truck. We didn't drive to Hawaii but we did drive to Alaska. I spent my summers living vicariously through my son until he became a teenager. Then I realized I'd better get out of his face so he could enjoy his teens. That's when I started looking for something to do.

Back then newsletters were in vogue so I said to Jack, 'Maybe we could do some kind of newsletter or something that would talk about finances and health.' Those seemed to be two areas that we were particularly interested in for women and they were subjects women shied away from.

As we started talking about it and deciding on specific editorial, the project kept growing and wound up becoming a regular publication versus a newsletter. We bought twenty-five thousand names of women and used Morris County as a hub and officially launched the publication targeting women, who at that point, had fifty thousand dollars in personal income and family incomes of at least one hundred thousand dollars.

There was a lot of excitement about this new magazine

about women with corporate, financial and entrepreneurial backgrounds because the idea had never surfaced before our publication. After we launched, NJ BIZ started featuring women on the cover of their publication. It was clear to us that we'd intuitively carved a new niche for women in business and we had no idea how big that simple idea would become over the years.

I Watched My Father Work Three Jobs

The intuitive piece probably has something to do with DNA. For example, my father was a milkman, a janitor and a landscaper all at the same time. Growing up we saw adults around us doing whatever needed to be done to survive. There was no discussion about it because they just made things happen. So, I believe the role-modeling shows you early on that you have to keep going and not stop so that you can survive and make ends meet.

Sometimes You Eat from Paycheck to Paycheck

My parents didn't receive a paycheck every Friday so my mother would not let us go in the refrigerator since every meal was planned out. Growing up with that mindset made me a little insecure whenever things got a little tight for Jack and me. I watched my parents fight about not having enough money because only one of my father's businesses paid him a regular salary. When you grow up with that mindset you develop the toughness as a leader so that you don't cave in during those times when you do have to eat from paycheck to paycheck. You become very resourceful and learn how to stretch things out so they last. That's even true when it comes to funding business ideas and projects.

A Mindset to Succeed

Our biggest challenge with *Garden State Woman* was always funding and we constantly looked for outside resources. Funding might easily be the number one challenge for most leaders.

Getting the right people for your team is another big challenge because you want people who will buy into the passionate part of the vision. I found that to be especially true when it came to hiring women for the business. We tried to hire women but with little funding we had to ask them to volunteer until we could pay them a salary. Most of the women we offered that deal to just couldn't accept it because they needed a steady income for their families. Also, we found that a lot of the women we tried to recruit were the primary caretakers for their children and that impacted their ability to work the kind of hours we needed them to work. So, with definite limitations in terms of funding and staffing we had to keep convincing ourselves that if we hung in there we'd reap the benefits over time. We were right about that once we found our own niche.

Be True to Your Own Definition

Finding your leadership niche is not easy, especially for women in leadership. Since launching Garden State Woman there were so many women who said, 'Oh, don't ever work with your husband.' I understood where they were coming from because in those cases you don't get a break from each other. Learning how to work well together in business and still enjoying a happy marriage is a learning process.

I tried to model that kind of message editorially through *Garden State Woman*. We would do cover stories about women who had to navigate between one thing and another. What we found our readers saying was something like, 'If she can do it, I can do it.' Our role-modeling served to remove excuses because we helped women realize they can do whatever they put their minds to do if it's in their DNA to get the thing done.

Press Re-Start if You Need to

I don't give in to fear because I'm committed to make things succeed. Other women leaders also have to be bold enough to be completely who they are. The worst thing that can happen is that we'll try something that won't work out the way we intended and we have to press re-start. Jack and I need more years for some do-overs because that's just how we're wired.

Mr. Jack Killion is a business executive with over thirty-five years of successful entrepreneurial experience, and he is the Founder & Managing Partner of Eagle Rock Diversified Fund, a fund of hedge funds now in its fourteenth year (www.eaglerockfund.com). Mr. Killion is also the Co-Founder of Bluestone + Killion, a company that provides networking and client development training and coaching to major professional firms and corporations. He offers strategic advisory guidance to leaders of and investors in early stage, high potential enterprises (www.bluestonekillion.com). Other achievements include heading several diverse businesses such as *Harper's Magazine* as turn around, interim management; *Country Music Magazine* as Founder and Publisher; *Killion Extruders* (industrial equipment manufacturing) as Owner & CEO; *Wireless for the Corporate User Magazine & Events Company* as Co-Founder, Publisher & Editor; *KBO* as Founder & General Partner (raise venture capital & consult with investors in emerging companies); *MBK* as Co-Founder (real estate development in Florida); *Walnut Farm* as Owner & Trainer (thoroughbred race horse breeding & racing stable), and *Information & Communications Technology Fund* as Co-Founder. Mr. Killion has evaluated thousands of deals and consulted with leaders & owners of hundreds of emerging companies in different countries and in diverse industries around the world. He raised equity and debt and sold, merged, re-structured, turned around and bought companies. Mr. Killion is the author of several articles for entrepreneurs and he is a frequent and sought after guest speaker for entrepreneurial and business events. Mr. Killion also headed the U.K. division of a public British technology company and two U.S. based divisions of Thermal Scientific, a public U.K. technology company. In addition to serving for two years in the U.S. Army, Mr. Killion consulted with heads of Fortune 500s while with McKinsey & Company. His clients included AMEX, CBS, Columbia Records, Port of Philadelphia, Burlington-Great Northern Railway, City of New York, and others. Mr. Killion earned a Master of Science degree from MIT Sloan School of Business, a Bachelor of Science degree in Mechanical Engineering from Yale University, and he is an MBA Adjunct Professor at Rutgers University, Montclair State University and Fairleigh Dickinson University. He also serves as Educational Counselor at MIT in Northern New Jersey, Advisor at SIFE Program at Centenary College, and he is currently developing the MIT-Sloan Business School Community of Northern New Jersey. Mr. Killion is presently a trustee and advisor with the Park Avenue Club, Medical Missions for Children, Garden State Woman Education Foundation and Sheffield Capital. He was previously a trustee with various U.S. and European corporations. He also worked in the U.K. for Elliot Automation, a British firm, and in France for BAT, a

French firm. Mr. Killion's business repertoire includes extensive international travel for the purpose of developing global business opportunities in a range of niche businesses. He resides in northern New Jersey with his wife, Judy Chapman Killion. They have a son, Johnathan, who graduated from Delbarton Independent College Preparatory School for Boys and Georgetown University.

Pictured above is gutsy husband and wife team Mr. Jack Killion and Ms. Judy Chapman Killion on Sunday, February 16, 2014 during their book interview.

Mr. Jack Killion

Be Willing to Do Things

Being a gutsy leader means being willing to do things. I don't really think of anything we've done as particularly gutsy because I believe that anybody could have done what we've done. I find that a lot of people plan to do things but they never act on their plans.

I teach an MBA program and tell the students, 'I wouldn't spend all of my time simply planning, I'd spend most of my time *doing*. Things will never be exactly what you expect them to be when you start out so you might as well keep things moving until you get the end result.'

Be Ready to Experience Different Leadership Moments

Judy and I have had a variety of leadership moments. *Garden State Woman* is essentially Judy's project. Also, Judy ran our farm simultaneously with starting the magazine. We bred and trained race horses and Judy's role was to run the farm, which is a big role. I've had my own projects for almost forty years.

The trigger that led me to go off on my own was when the large management consulting firm I worked for started talking to me about becoming a partner. I wasn't convinced I wanted to be a partner. The night they started talking to me about becoming a partner was when I called Judy and said, 'I just made two decisions.' She said, 'What?' I said, 'I'm buying a race horse.' She said, 'When?' Because we didn't have any money at the time I said, 'As soon as I can find a cheap race horse.' She said, 'What else did you decide?' I said, 'I'm quitting my job.' She said, 'When?' I said, 'Tomorrow.' She said, 'To do what?' I said, 'I'm not sure.'

Be Clear About What You Want and Don't Want

I didn't want the company to think I was interested in being a partner so I thought I'd better head off their offer from the start. The next morning I told the person I reported to that I would be wrapping up all of my projects and leaving the company. I stood by my word and stayed for a few months to clean up the projects I was working on. I left and have been on my own ever since.

Trying Something Totally New Takes Guts

I sort of have the DNA to successfully run small businesses. After I left the management consulting firm I picked up two partners pretty quickly and we spent five years trying to raise money for small companies. We raised money for *Rolling Stone Magazine* and that's how we got interested in publishing. By the end of five years my partners and I had probably looked at a thousand deals so I really got good at looking at deals. Unfortunately, we didn't make any money when we first started out because of how tough it is to make money raising capital for small businesses. We found that most of the small companies we ran into weren't that good so one day I said to my two partners, 'This is fun but if we're so good at looking at deals then we should raise our own money and start our own business.' They agreed.

I wanted to start a financial services business, an idea that I had tested and thought would've worked. One of my partners believed we should take advantage of what we learned at *Rolling Stone Magazine* and start the first national country music magazine. Eventually, that's what we did but there was a lot of debate about it at first. We debated over whether to go with my idea to start a financial services business or my partner's idea to start a national country magazine. With his idea we'd have to raise half a million dollars. With my idea I didn't think we'd have to raise any money at all.

One day I saw an article in *The New York Times* about *Harper's Magazine* being in financial trouble so I called my partner and said, 'I'll make you a deal. Let's call the guys who own Harper's and see if we can get them to hire us to turn Harper's around. The magazine would have to agree to put up half a million dollars but they would own half of our start-up country music magazine.' We made that call and we convinced the *Minneapolis Star Tribune* to hire a publisher, which was us, and they gave us a check for half a million dollars for the start-up magazine. My partners and I saw an opportunity and we went for it even though none of us had any experience in running a national country music magazine.

Shift Gears to Seize Opportunities

Starting *Country Music Magazine* is an example of seeing an opportunity and thinking outside of the box to seize that opportunity. When my partners and I received the five hundred thousand dollar check we had a nice little spiral-bound business plan. As I now tell my MBA students, 'A business plan doesn't have much to do with what you do the next day after you've sealed the deal.'

On my way home from getting the check I decided to try to find a local country music bar to go to since I'd never been in one before and didn't know anything about country music. I stopped at a biker's bar near the Meadowlands in Carlstadt. As I sat there in my nice little business suit the female bartender came over to me and said, 'What are you doing in here? You're so out of place.' I told her what I was doing and she got excited because she thought the idea of a national country magazine was great. The bartender's husband was playing music behind me on a little platform and came down during a break to meet me.

The bartender's husband said, 'This is fantastic. We've never had a quality national publication for our industry. We close the bar at one o'clock and we live right upstairs.

You should stay until we close so you can come upstairs and tell us more about the magazine.' I stayed and went upstairs to their apartment and just started taking notes about important people I should talk to in Nashville, who should go on the first issue's cover, who could write content, where to get information, etc. At around three o'clock in the morning the couple called Les Paul the guitar player and told him to come right over so he could hear about a start-up country music magazine. Les came over and played his guitar while he talked to us. We talked about the new magazine until about seven-thirty in the morning.

I'm sure the magazine would have been successful even if I hadn't stopped at the biker's bar, but it would've been a totally different kind of company. Having the courage to make that one stop took me down the right road because I saw an opportunity, went to a bar, kept my mouth shut and listened to words of wisdom. The magazine did better than my partners and I ever imagined it would.

There Will Be Challenges Even When There's Success

Aside from getting enough funding getting good people was a challenge for my partners and me. When my father died I was running *Harper's Magazine* and *Country Music Magazine*. My father died on a Saturday in February and he left behind a failing manufacturing company. I went to the company on Saturday afternoon because I had not been involved in the business since we hadn't spoken with each other for ten years.

I went into my father's old office and looked through the checkbooks. Things were a total mess so I called his accountant and told him my father had passed away. The accountant told me that he and my father had talked about bankrupting the company. I said, 'You can't do that if I understand what I'm looking at. My mother's house is part of everything.' I wound up working at the manufacturing company the following Monday. So, it was two magazines, a manufacturing company, and I still worked on our farm because the farm was owned by my father.

All of a sudden I found myself running four different businesses at the same time. I tried to hire an experienced person because it was impossible for me to physically be at the manufacturing company, which was in a deep crisis. I tried to hire someone with experience in manufacturing but had no luck. I met a number of professional candidates who talked to me about employment contracts and health benefits. I had to say to each one of them, 'Pal, I don't even know if this company can make it to Friday so I can't even talk to you about salary or benefits.'

Search for Who Wants Your Coaching

There was a young guy who already worked for the company. He had no educational background but he was very good with his hands, and he was as close to what I was looking for as I could find. I saw him as someone I could develop so I called him into my office one day after I'd been there for a couple of weeks. I said, 'Hey, Bob. You know what? I'd like to try to save this company and get it going but I need someone who can be my eyes and ears since I'll be in New York most of my time. I'd like to put the effort into training you to be my number two guy.'

He didn't even hesitate before saying, 'I don't want to do that. I don't want to be under the kind of pressure you're under and I don't want to work like you work. I'm happy coming in at seven-thirty in the morning and going home at four o'clock in the afternoon.' I said, 'Are you sure?' He said, 'Yeah. I'm sure.' I never had another conversation with him about it and he stayed with the company for about ten years content with making a very low salary.

The opposite of that was when I called Montclair State University because they had a plastics program. I said, 'I'm trying to find somebody I can develop into my number two guy and you've got a plastics program. Do you have any really bright young guy who's graduating who I should speak with?' They told me they had one guy named Keith. When I met Keith he and I didn't hit it off because I thought he had a big chip on his shoulder even though he was clearly smart and capable.

Keith and I met several times and I finally offered him the job for around twelve thousand dollars. He told me he had been offered twenty thousand dollars by IBM so I told him he should take the job with IBM. I said, 'Take the job at IBM for twenty thousand dollars or come work here and be trained by me. I don't even know if this manufacturing company will make it but if you stay here, at some point I guarantee you that you'll be able to start your own business. You won't be able to do that if you go to IBM.' Keith came on board with me and stayed for around twelve years until one day he came in and said, 'I have bad news.' I said, 'What's the bad news? Are you starting your own company?' He said, 'Yeah.' I said, 'That's good news. I told you you'd do that. You'll do well.'

I believe leaders have to be unconventional and try to find the right people. For example, when I trained horses at the race track there was a trainer who was really struggling. He was married and had two kids but struggled to the point of having to sleep in his car at the track because he couldn't afford to go back and forth from home to the track. When there was a break in the season he asked me if he could come work with me in my factory. I said, 'You've got no background. I don't think it would be fair for me to bring you in while the company is still struggling just because you're my buddy from the racetrack.'

I told him he could come work for nothing and I'd train him even though I'd expect him to be out looking for a job most days. I told him that while he worked for no salary and got trained by me he would be building up his resume and seeing if he really liked the work. He came and he spent about three months with me. At the end of three months he had to either go back to training horses or continue at the factory. He said, 'I'd like to stay here. I think I could be pretty good at this.' I said, 'I agree.' We negotiated a deal and I paid him retroactively based on the deal we'd just cut. I wanted to see whether he would do the job for no pay. He stayed with me for over ten years and is now earning about two hundred and fifty thousand dollars a year in sales in the plastics industry. I believe that being unconventional and taking chances to bring the right people on board pays off.

Be a Thinker and Take Chances

I probably think twenty hours a day, seven days a week. It's easy to do that when you're involved in multiple businesses at the same time. I'm always trying to make things better, avoid mistakes, set some priorities and push ahead because I don't believe there are too many things a motivated person can't accomplish. It doesn't matter how big the objective is or how limited resources are, I think if you're generally capable and motivated you can reach your goals.

I've been to the White House three times. With Presidents Nixon, Carter, and Obama. Just by trying. With *Country Music Magazine* I tried to figure out what my partners and I could do with the first issue so we sent a copy to President Nixon because we knew he was into country music.

As a leader, when you're asked to take a different leadership position or some new responsibilities you should always say 'Yes.' After you sign on then you can think about how to get the work done. Just raise your hand and say 'Yes.' Don't spend too much time thinking about it because that's when fear has an opportunity to creep in and disable you. Dive in and take small steps to get to where you need to be.

Assemble a Coaching and Advisory Team

It's important for leaders to take incremental steps and adjust as they go. For instance, when our son was about to graduate from college he assembled an advisory team of core people and I was one of the team members. The team advised our son on his resume, we put him in touch with people, and we coached him on how to interview.

After he graduated we talked and I told him that he should put together a life coaching team consisting of a lawyer, an accountant, an insurance person, and someone for wealth management. We interviewed two people from each category and one of the wealth managers said to Jonathan, 'What do you want to be when you grow up?' Jonathan said, 'I want to be able to tell good stories.' He learned that from Judy and me and he knows that a leader can't tell good stories unless he or she has done good things.

Dr. Dharius Daniels is a cultural architect and trendsetter for his generation. He is an innovative leader, a strategic thinker, author, and an articulate and prolific preacher who is the Senior Pastor and Founder of _Kingdom Church_. At two locations in Ewing and Burlington, New Jersey, this is a vibrant ministry that impacts people of all ages, socioeconomic classes, and ethnic backgrounds. _"Our mission is to make disciples of Jesus Christ, our King, through seeking, shaping, serving, and sending. Since our inception we have witnessed thousands of lives touched, changed, transformed, and mended by the grace and to the glory of God. We are a non-denominational church that celebrates diversity. We believe you don't have to be this or that but we can be this and that. We invite you to experience our heartfelt worship, relevant ministry, breathtaking culture, and biblical teaching."_ Kingdom Church was founded in August of 2005 and currently has a rapidly growing congregation of several thousand members. Dr. Daniels developed the _Breathtaking Ministry_ concept, which describes the standard of excellence at Kingdom Church – a standard that is apparent in his commitment not only to ministry but also to education. The ministry has awarded $1,000 college book fund scholarships to graduating high school seniors since the inception of the ministry. To date, the church has awarded $100,000+ in scholarships to students who apply. Among Kingdom Church's global missions work is the adoption of a children's orphanage in Haiti. In addition to providing monthly financial support to the orphanage that includes providing the children and staff at the orphanage with clean, running water, Dr. Daniels, his family, and members of the congregation pay their own expenses to visit the orphanage three to four times every year to hand-deliver clothing, supplies and health care materials. Dr. Daniels has a heart for people so he led a *Wednesday Morning Prayer Call* in 2014 so that people around the world, particularly those who serve in the military and couldn't get to a regular church service could participate in a weekly, ten-minute conference call where Dr. Dharius taught and prayed for the callers. In 2015 Kingdom Church began live streaming of its Wednesday night and Sunday services at the Ewing campus (kcnj.org). Additionally in 2015, Dr. Dharius started the Thrive Ministry at Kingdom Church, which serves business owners and senior executives through monthly and quarterly teaching and networking sessions designed to help them thrive by doing ministry in the marketplace. Dr. Daniels earned a Bachelor of Arts degree in Political Science from Millsaps College in Jackson, Mississippi, a Master of Divinity degree from Princeton Theological Seminary in Princeton, New Jersey, and a Doctorate of Ministry degree from Fuller Theological Seminary in Pasadena, California. Dr. Daniels is the author of the book, *RePresent Jesus: Rethink Your Version of Christianity and Become More Like Christ*, which is available on Amazon and Barnes

& Noble online and at retail locations. Dr. Daniels is known both nationally and internationally for his versatile gifts, and he is a sought after speaker and presenter at events and training sessions that are hosted by seminaries and churches across the country. Dr. Daniels serves on the Board of Directors for the National Association of Evangelicals, and he is the President and Founder of the Kingdom Mentorship Network, which provides coaching and training to pastors and church planters. He and his wife, Shameka, are the proud parents of two young sons, Dharius Seth and Gabriel Micah Daniels.

Dr. Dharius Daniels, Pastor
Intuitive and Courageous

Being gutsy isn't always *feeling* gutsy. Two specific words come to my mind when I hear the word gutsy – intuitive and courageous. I believe intuition is a gift and that every human being has it. Sometimes we sense the necessity to make decisions and certain moves. Being courageous thrusts gutsy leaders into acting on their intuition even when we are not sure of what might work and what might not work.

Highly intuitive people act on intuition even though their intuition is not always trustworthy or accurate. Any gutsy transformational leader will probably admit that he or she made bad decisions about staff hires and about other things that the leader initially felt very good about. That's where the transformational part comes in – gutsy leaders have to know when it's time to make transformative changes even after they're put themselves out there and made a decision that might not have worked out as well as expected. For gutsy leaders, transformation is almost an inevitable result even when that leader might not necessarily be transformational by nature.

Be Clear about Your Purpose

I decided to make radical transformational changes when I recognized a problem where tradition within the Church wasn't reaching the current century's demographic. Being part of that generational demographic gave me a personal connection to the problem. During that time I didn't feel my moves were gutsy as much as they were a sense of call to duty to live out my purpose.

That generational demographic problem gave me clarity about my purpose when I was only about twenty-two or twenty-three years old. When I was twenty-six years old I acted on that clarity. I perceived that the dominant approaches in my field were failing to reach an entire generation, including me, and I felt completely connected to the problem.

I researched and thought through ways to actually do something about the problem and I didn't know how good I'd be at it being only twenty-six. I can honestly say that I got clarity that the historically dominant approach that was taken in the faith-based community was not reaching my generational demographic and I wanted to be part of the solution here locally in New Jersey.

Being clear on your purpose means knowing the difference between talent, passion, and call. Discerning the difference between those three things will give you so much clarity when it comes to opportunities that you are and are not supposed to take advantage of. One of my doctoral professors says, 'You'll know you hit your sweet spot when all three of those things intersect.'

Reflecting back on our start, I would say that what I did was gutsy, but at that time I just said to myself, *This generational demographic issue is a problem...things as they are aren't working.'* I had no idea exactly what I would do or how I wanted to get to where I knew we needed to go as a radically different church.

Have the Self-Confidence to Go Up Against Giants

I was a bit naïve when I started out and that actually served me well because I don't think being naïve is always a bad thing. For example, David in the bible had to be a little bit naïve to go up against the giant Goliath. If I had completely thought through everything I was up against when we were starting out I might not have taken the step to start Kingdom Church and take this particular approach with ministry. For me, the kingdom reward outweighed the reward for me personally so I was focused on that.

I'm not sure if I recall everything I experienced back then but I know that sometimes I was certainly more confident than at other times. Even though I'm a pastor I still lean heavily on my mental side to make decisions because I believe leaders need emotional sobriety in order to lead effectively. Leaders cannot become intoxicated by their emotions. I'm not suggesting that everything a gutsy leader will do will always be rational. That's not the case because I don't think that starting this church was rational. If I thought about everything from a rational perspective I probably would not have started this church because the idea was so completely different from anything I'd ever seen before. We had to build the plane as we flew it because there was no model that I knew of.

I became so consumed with solving the generational demographic issue that a lot of the concern I probably *should* have had was superseded by thoughtful actions. I didn't have a Plan B so if this model didn't work I would have had to figure out what to do next. Within this pastoral office I have a Plan B rolling around for everything so not having one for the church model was unusual for me. I was just so focused on having the guts to put all of my effort into making sure I did the best I could to confront what was to me a giant of an issue in my field.

Be Strong, Courageous, and Decisive

As a pastor the first thing I do when I'm anxious about a giant issue is pray. I've discovered that I don't have a lot of control over my emotions but I do have control over how I manage them, so I manage the emotions through prayer. For instance, I can't decide if I'm going to feel anxious or afraid about something or someone. I know I need God's help with that. The book of Joshua talks about being strong and courageous and sometimes as a leader you have to *be* strong even when you don't *feel* strong.

It's also important for leaders to have inner circles of friends who serve as peer mentors and can speak to you on every level. Those individuals can be transparent with you and speak to you in ways that people you're leading generally choose not to. Sometimes talking through my emotions allows me the space to acknowledge fear and own the fact that it exists in certain situations. I trust my mentor circle to provide me with alternative perspectives to address fear, stay focused, and make sound decisions.

Guard the Trust of Others

Just as my mentor circle earned my trust, as a leader I know that I have to earn and guard the trust of everyone in my congregation and on my staff. That's actually a challenge not unique to my pastoral office. For example, I saw this with the BP Motor spill when a CEO had to resign and he wasn't even in the country when the spill occurred. As a leader everything might not be your fault but everything about the organization is your responsibility. Leading with that in mind helps earn people's trust.

In my pastoral office people expect this to be a place they can trust. I believe that's why there's so much mistrust and vitriol when people in my position misuse and abuse the trust of those they lead. People hope and expect that if there's nowhere else to trust I can trust *here*. For example, when parents come to Kingdom Church and leave their kids in Children's Church so they can participate in a worship service, for the most part they're leaving their kids with me even though I don't work in Children's Church. Eventually they get to know the youth workers but some of them don't even know who our youth pastor is. The parents trust that as the pastor I have ensured that all the necessary standards and procedures are in place for their children to be properly cared for. The reality is that I know our youth pastor but I don't know everybody he works with. If something were to happen it might not be my fault but it would be my responsibility. I do a lot to guard the trust of people.

Avoid Moving at the Speed of Profit and Be Authentic

Something else that's helped us gain the trust of people is the fact that we don't move at the speed of profit, we move at the speed of trust here. We can go only as fast as our trust level exists with the congregation. Creating and building a culture of trust at Kingdom Church has always been at the top of my priority list because one thing I recognized among my generation was that there was high distrust regarding churches. The mistrust was not just with church leadership but with what Christianity appeared to have morphed into in general. We felt that we could not trust the church with our worst selves.

I knew that in order to reach that generational demographic we'd have to be authentic. Not perfect but completely authentic because in being authentic we would become trustworthy. We've spent a good amount of time and energy creating a trusting culture of authenticity, but that hasn't been easy.

Essential Things Might Not Be Easy Things to Achieve

I don't think anything that I do is particularly easy but teaching is probably the easiest thing that I do. I'm much more comfortable teaching than I am with preaching. My teaching approach involves me being authentically me but I deliver *me* differently based on the context in which I'm called to serve. I don't believe the goal is for me to feel fulfilled or get everything out of me that's in me. The goal is for me to serve people I'm called to serve.

Take for example a sermon series I did about life. I taught a sermon on decision making. Contextually, I know one thing that culturally we all could do better decision making from a biblical perspective. I know based on reports I get every week from the person who does our counseling that I'm looking at a lot of crises that are not the sole result of immorality. The crises we learn about are sometimes a result of poor decision making so I did a lesson on decision making.

You might have somebody who's trying to figure out whether to stay with someone who's beating him or her and the way you deliver information to the person is to have the necessary content drive the delivery style. Switching up on the style might pose challenges but doing so is a necessity if the message is going to be relevant.

Assess What People Need and Coach Them on Those Areas

I believe leaders absolutely have to conduct needs assessments if they want to be relevant. In different contexts you go about gathering data in different ways but here in a religious context we have to be a bit more probing as we're gathering information about what we should be focusing on. I can't use surveys because people generally respond to surveys based on self-diagnostics, which are not necessarily reflective of the complete picture.

We teach that The Gospel helps us see the big picture so we can identify what our needs and problem areas are. We also teach here that the bible shines a light on areas that we need improvement in, which negatively impact our lives and the lives of others in dramatic ways that we might not even be cognizant of. For us, the needs assessments are based on two things. One, they're based on what people articulate to us, and two, on what we've been able to discern and assess in our interactions with different people.

Some people come in and say, 'I have men problems' so we assess and probe by asking the right questions and we help identify that those individuals really have decision making problems and they're choosing the wrong people. Then, we go about teaching and coaching to help them develop more sound decision making skills.

I believe every leader should conduct regular needs

assessments with the people they lead by building relationships with them and engaging in straight talk conversations with them about what's really going on. By doing that the leader helps solidify an overall healthy climate and culture within the organization, which then gives the leader the ability to focus more on embracing his or her gutsy leadership role.

Embrace Your Personal Wiring

I am wired to be strong-willed. I'll give a realistic picture of what I mean by that because I haven't seen that level of transparency shared in a lot of leadership books.

Rick Warren wrote great books like, *The Purpose-Driven Life* and *The Purpose-Driven Church* and in the books he wrote about all of the great stuff he'd done with his church. After hearing his presentation at a leadership conference I got a much clearer picture about what it actually took for his church to accomplish all that it did. For instance, it took them ten years to build a new facility and they encountered all kinds of major trials and obstacles along the way. They walked on the land, prayed on the land, and believed God for the land. They were still denied the rights to build on the land so they bought more land.

During my self-reflections and conversations with the team about Kingdom Church's projects and initiatives, we got further clarity about our building efforts. We'd initially thought our building project over a *few* years had been an eternity. But, ten years?! Rick Warren's transparency about his church's process helped us greatly.

So, during my self-reflection I admitted to myself that I'm strong-willed and impatient about certain things related to me fulfilling my purpose. I don't know many people who are strong-willed by choice but we're strong-willed because we have to be regarding things that even appear to be hindering the progress of purpose fulfillment. For example, part of me starting Kingdom Church was not wanting to wait five years in my previous church environment to see if the leadership would make adjustments in order to meet the needs of its multi-generational demographics. So, I'd say that although I'm strong-willed and impatient, I'm very strategic about it.

Strategic Leadership

Every aspect of our leadership here is strategic. For us, we're particularly strategic about what we say and do regarding the culture we're trying to create here. We want a culture where every demographic feels a sense of being at home. For instance, for some other churches when they tell people to 'Come as you are' they mean people should dress down. We believe that alone doesn't create a cultural comfort for the person who chooses to express himself or herself differently.

We're very intentional about our culture building strategy with our staff and leaders so we ensure that even our look reflects the type of diversity we're attempting to draw. That means we're intentional about who we put on the stage and when different people are put on stage because we believe that when you diversify your stage you diversify your church.

We have one choir that includes the young, middle-aged and elderly, not because churches are supposed to have a choir but because there are demographics in our congregation who are ministered to by choirs. We believe that what you do on your church's stage says a lot about what happens in the church as a whole and we strategically make decisions to address the needs of our diverse and multi-generational demographics.

Even in the way that we make decisions that impact the church we are strategic. We think through every decision. That's not to say that it's always the right strategy. But, we're thinking strategically, which has served us well in allowing us to be very creative in how we deliver our ministry.

Creativity Still Needs Timelines

We have monthly creative meetings here where I'll gather with some of the *creatives* on the team to spend four or five hours analyzing what we did the month before, and planning what we want to do in the upcoming months. This includes timelines for the different series I'll be teaching, the songs that will be sung to compliment the lesson series, operational things about each of the services, staging design, what our attire will be, what advertising promos we'll use, etc.

Because we do heavy media here I always ask the creatives in media and marketing if what we're planning is too much for us to handle. For example, are six videos over the next two months too unrealistic based on the technology and manpower that we have? When we leave the meeting room after establishing firm deadlines for the actionable items we talked about, as the senior leader of this organization I'm not too understanding or patient when those agreed upon deadlines aren't met to the high standards we try to maintain here. I'm not as patient because I asked if meeting our goals by an established timeline would be too difficult based on whatever variables. Since I don't work in the field of media or marketing I rely on our experts to help me as the leader to develop and stick to realistic timelines for delivery. We understand that we might have to tweak things along the way because we have a culture here of making adjustments to things based on current needs so that we avoid becoming a church that's limited by tradition.

Culture of Incessant Tinkering

When we strategically plan, some of our action steps are the direct result of turns we've had to make. For instance, we might run into a wall and find that what we'd planned can't happen because of some new development so we need to take a different route. I'd bet that at times my team second guesses my leadership because I'm one who's always adapting based on needs. That's why I believe it's so important for leaders to constantly communicate to those being led the necessity of fluidity and making adaptive changes to help the organization's people succeed through any unexpected obstacles. Leaders should also spend a lot of time and energy giving the assurance that one way or another the organization will reach its goals despite factors and variables beyond leadership's control. That way, people can more readily attribute the necessity of taking alternative routes to the variables and not to a lack of effective, strategic and responsive leadership. We regularly communicate to the congregation and to every new and existing team member that we have a culture of incessant tinkering.

We find that communicating about the tinkering culture helps keep our expectations authentically clear to avoid people becoming frustrated because they believe they're not doing a good job. We're always tweaking and fixing things at every level of our organization to make sure that what's being done addresses current versus past needs and capacity levels. We believe here that mediocrity is bad stewardship of a person's potential. We don't think that everyone will excel at everything, but we do believe every human being can excel at something. As a leadership team we adjust when needed to help people invest in and cultivate their gifts, skills and capacity levels.

I believe that as an organization we're getting better at that as time goes along by constantly analyzing abstract things and concretizing them until we identify why we're not meeting our goals. Once something has been concretized and is still not what we want, we bust it up again until we get it right based on the high standards we've set at our church.

No Room for Mediocrity

For leaders, building right the first time is always less messy and less expensive than remodeling. Leadership teams might have to tear things down to dig deep and see what excellence should look like. One thing we do here is take something abstract like 'What is a good video?' I'll then find a video I believe meets the excellence standard. As I'm sharing the video with a creative I'll say, 'Do you see the lighting? There are no shadows. Our video has shadows. Do you see the various angles with the shot? Do you see how thick our letters are versus the size of the lettering on the exemplary video? This is the quality of video we're trying for here.'

Reaching for high standards in everything we do happens rather organically here. We make sure of that by having new staff members complete memorandums of understanding with their immediate supervisors. We're a staff-led church so it's important that everyone flow with one vision and mission for maintaining excellence at our church. We believe that if we get mediocrity out of those who are leading then you get mediocrity out of the organization. We're able to keep everyone on one page by requiring that all new hires have conversations with their supervisors regarding what acceptable performance looks like. During the conversation we ask the new hires to take notes and then create a document that becomes the memorandum of understanding, which they're later able to rehash with their supervisors until a final document is agreed upon. Then, both the new hire and the supervisor sign it and place the memorandum in the person's personnel file.

We also give specific and targeted feedback, particularly about the areas that we believe are more consequential to the success of the organization. For example, we'll say to the praise team, 'Hey, you guys aren't moving enough. It's not that you need to move better than you're moving, we just need you to move with more energy.' Giving specific feedback also helps leaders share the organization's overall vision with the people they're leading.

Cast the Vision So There's Buy-In

Vision casting is critical for gutsy leaders. I'll speak in the context of pastors since that's my role. Each month I meet with all of the staff for vision casting. Once we cast the vision and allow time for people to ask questions about anything they need clarified, I then put the onus of sharing and carrying out that vision on the team. It's up to the team to determine how each person can best capture parts of the vision that they will ultimately be held accountable for. This requires that leaders, their teams, and everyone being led establish an organizational culture that is open, transparent and completely authentic.

Focus on Authenticity

Gutsy leaders tend to embrace and celebrate their uniqueness, which is one of the things that makes them authentically gutsy. Problems arise when our human pride steps in and makes it difficult for us as frontline leaders to acknowledge when we're not really being ourselves. There can be a temptation to emulate what leaders see that they believe represents true leadership success even when what they see doesn't match their individual gifts, talents and personality wiring. I believe a leader's effectiveness becomes evident when he or she authentically allows those three attributes to live out in their leadership moments.

To manage your moment and handle your moment you've got to be authentically you. I often ask pastors I mentor, 'How do you lead? How are you wired to lead?' I remind them that if they try to lead the way that I or someone else leads it won't work because they might not be wired to lead that way. For example, I naturally think strategically and if you don't you might have to hire someone or find a volunteer who does. Just admitting that can help a leader remain authentic.

Number one for leaders is for them to be authentic. Number two is for them to lead with emotional sobriety and let the emotions remain in the car that can't drive. I coach pastors about how emotions can impact business decisions they make even about how large to build their churches. I'll ask, 'Why are you building that big?' I believe it's about more than winning souls when a pastor's focus is merely on building a big building. The focus might have more to do with the way the building makes the person feel about him or herself, and about the admiration they get from others because of the big building.

If leaders don't effectively identify and manage their emotional issues they can easily become emotional weaknesses that eventually manifest somewhere in the organization. Once that happens it becomes that much more difficult for leaders to be authentically themselves because their emotional perspectives might be off.

Start With Perspective

I believe everything begins with a leader's perspective but I've found that some pastors have difficulty understanding that because of the way they perceive the office of the pastor. I'll be very frank and practical and not spiritualize my perspective. This church 'train-wrecking' is not in my best interest. Even on my most non-spiritual day I want what's best for this organization and I want the best people around me giving me the best advice on how to succeed. Failing at this would also not be in the best interest of God's call on my life. When the rubber meets the road that's how I see it. I believe when leaders develop that perspective they create a culture among their staff and the people they lead of frankness, honesty and respect. That helps build strong organizational relationships where leaders get everybody on board saying, 'This thing train-wrecking is not in *our* best interest.'

I've seen where the success of an organization is just not perceived that way by some leaders. I believe my identity isn't wrapped up in my pastoral role because I've always had a variety of leadership interests and experiences. For instance, I played basketball in college, was in a fraternity, and I was class president in high school. So, for me getting credit and glory about my pastoral image has never been my priority. Other leaders may have had different experiences, and for those individuals it could be more challenging to resist wrapping their identity into their roles. That might make it difficult for them to accept criticism or feedback when their perspective is self-serving, and they actually might not know what they're doing well and what they're doing poorly.

Know What You Do Well

As a leader, when you know what you do well you don't mind surrounding yourself with others who do other things even better than you do. We invite people to be on our board of directors because they're smart and skilled in different areas. That means that as a pastor I don't have to know everything about business and the law and I can focus on what I'm purposed to do, which includes standing before large and small groups of people to teach them the principles of kingdom living. I believe we've done a good job of creating that type of culture here. Our CFO and others on the team who have expertise in different areas can yank our coattails if there's ever any indication that our vision is becoming self-serving, which could bleed the church.

Create a Culture of Transparent Discourse

Being able to create a culture where honest and transparent conversations happen with regularity and normalcy is something that perhaps every gutsy leader wants. The danger of not having that in a religious context is that the consequences reflect dealing with people's souls and not just with their employment. We strongly believe there are eternal ramifications at stake so we have to do the best job we can to manage the dynamic of transparency.

We've worked hard at maintaining a culture where even

when our leadership team members disagree about something we can respect and appreciate everyone else's perspective. We would say, 'We understand your perspective but we don't agree with it and we each have a right to have different perspectives.' Candor, openness and listening ears are requirements for every conversation that occurs here because we recognize that if that doesn't happen both the individuals who disagree and those who are observers will probably all pull back and withdraw to their separate corners. As leaders, we're challenged with giving and getting feedback and then stepping back to let the feedback run its course. That's a leadership strategy that comes with experience.

The Value of Experience

When I was a young start-up pastor I didn't appreciate or know the value of experience. No matter how much you read or how much counsel you surround yourself with as a new leader, there are some leadership lessons you'll learn only through experience if you have the personal resilience to stay the course through hard lessons. For example, one area we've struggled with is assembling the right team. Jesus got it right. He picked the right twelve for His team even though he had one bad apple (Judas).

In the area of putting together the right team I'd honestly say we have just stunk it up partly because we used to focus on hiring managers versus leaders. Early on we recruited and hired based on skill and character since we wanted high moral character and competence. What we found was that when you have an organization that takes a unique approach to anything you need more than skill. As we became more experienced we saw that chemistry is what you have to take into consideration when you're assembling a leadership team. It took us years to understand that the right fit for a position in this multi-generational and diverse culture is just as important as high moral character and skill.

Guts to Be Radically Different

I have strong philosophical differences on orthodoxy with some of my trusted mentors who are of high moral character. That means there are some church practices they engage in because they trace orthodoxy back to the orthodox church while I trace orthodoxy back to the scriptures. As a result, we do some things radically differently here and some of our methods might not just be seen as radical but at times as being arrogant and even sacrilegious.

Being different in this field is rarely embraced and the fruitfulness of what we do here is sometimes perceived by outsiders as a lowering of standards. I imagine there are churches that might not have had our experiences and don't share our philosophy. However, we try to maintain our own identity and remain faithful to what we believe we're called to do as a church. We do this without condemning or berating others who might see things differently. This might cause us to be misunderstood by some, but at the same time we believe we're appreciated by others.

Within the leadership network people say, 'This is going on in the Northeast? Tell us about it.' As a matter of fact, my book publishing deal with Charisma House came about because Kingdom Church was featured in an article in *Relevant Magazine*, specifically about our age diversity and our approach to ministry. Just by having the guts to lead a radically different church has not only grown a thriving church, but it's opened so many doors for members of our leadership team and our congregation at large.

Emphasize the DNA of Gutsy Leadership

The DNA concept of your book is an underemphasized leadership trait that distinguishes good leaders from great leaders. The distinction ties back to guts. How many people had amazing ideas but didn't follow through on them? It takes guts. Bill Gates and Steve Jobs exemplified guts when they branched out and built their empires.

I pray that God blesses you with this book project and that He invites providence and grace by putting you in the path of the right people at the right time to get the book in the hands of many different people as soon as possible.

This is something for you guys to think about: do gutsy

leaders require a unique type of followship? If I'm becoming a part of any organization is it helpful for me to know that it's being led by a gutsy transformational leader before I sign on? How might the gutsy leader's attributes impact me as a member of the team? Or, if I'm the gutsy leader should it impact the criteria I use to assemble my team? What type of character traits does someone need to have to fit within the culture of the organization I'm leading? It's possible that if you wait to see whether or not someone has *it* sometimes you may rob the person of an opportunity *to get it.* I believe the first place gutsy leadership should be revealed is in the ascension of the entire team. This would be a by-product of the success of a gutsy transformational leader.

I don't have the answer to those thoughts but maybe it's something to think through for the next book in this series.

Mr. Peter Grandich, renowned Wall Street guru, founded Peter Grandich & Company. He also co-founded a subsidiary company, Trinity Financial Sports & Entertainment Management Company, LLC with two-time Super Bowl champion New York Giant, Lee Rouson. Trinity provides business, retirement and estate planning to professional athletes, entertainers and the general public. Though Mr. Grandich never finished high school, he entered Wall Street in the mid-1980s with no formal education or training and within three years was appointed to the position of Vice President of Investment Strategy for a leading New York Stock Exchange member firm. Mr. Grandich would go on to hold positions as a market strategist, portfolio manager for four hedge funds, and head of a mutual fund that bore his name. His savvy abilities resulted in hundreds of media interviews with *Good Morning America, Neil Cavuto's Your World on Fox News, The Kudlow Report on CNBC, The Wall Street Journal, Barron's, Financial Post, Globe and Mail, US News & World Report, The New York Times, Business Week, MarketWatch, Business News Network*, and dozens of other entities. Mr. Grandich is a requested speaker and presenter at investment conferences around the globe. He has also edited numerous investment newsletters, and is one of the more sought after commentators about all things business. He is a member and supporter of the following organizations: National Association of Christian Financial Consultants, Athletes in Action, Fellowship of Christian Athletes, and Good News International Ministries. Through the Athletes & Business Alliance, Mr. Grandich assists with bible study and chapel services for the New York Giants and New York Yankees. He is also a member of the National Sports Marketing Network. He has served as the Editor and Publisher of *The Grandich Letter* since 1984. Mr. Grandich was appointed to the role of Senior Commentator for *Moneytalks.Net*, and is a regular guest market commentator on the *Michael Campbell Show*, Canada's most listened to financial talk show. In 2013, he founded the Athletes & Business Alliance (ABA). The ABA is a private organization of professional athletes and business executives who exchange ideas and build relationships with an emphasis on capitalizing on everyone's talents. A symbiotic organization, the ABA is a network of accomplished individuals who network in an environment focused on developing personal associations within a structured and supportive system of giving and receiving business. The ABA boasts a select membership of diverse senior-level executives, high-net-worth business owners, and both active and retired professional athletes, who by invitation only connect and network. Mr. Grandich believes that in order to achieve success, businesses must utilize effective marketing tools, secure new customers to generate repeat business, and provide superior customer service that engenders loyalty. The ABA provides an environment to do this and more. Mr. Grandich's autobiography, *Confessions of a Wall Street Whiz Kid*, was published in the fall of 2011 and a second edition was issued in 2014. The publication is available on Amazon.com. For more information visit the book's website: www.ConfessionsOfaWallStreetWhizKid.com. Mr. Grandich resides in New Jersey with his wife, Mary, and their daughter, Tara.

Peter Grandich

Willing to Take the Lumps

A gutsy leader is someone who doesn't operate within the confines of what the world thinks he or she should. The person is also willing to take the lumps for any bad decisions he or she makes. I've led by my gut instincts almost my entire career in forecasting and at times my observers viewed that as me not making traditional business moves.

For example, a former close friend was at one time perhaps one of the most renowned financial commentator in the country. Just around the time that my daughter was born I came to know Christ and decided to make Christ the driver of all of my business decisions. The business associate called my wife Mary and said that I was making a huge mistake by tying my faith to my business career. I did tie my faith to my business dealings and shortly thereafter the friendship ended. While I believe the bible includes an enormous amount of teachings about finances, I learned that most people didn't appreciate me tying my religious beliefs to my business dealings. At times this clash in beliefs impacted my mental state and forced me to make tough decisions as a well-known business leader.

From the Abyss to the Sweet Spot

Mentally I'd really been to the edge of the abyss by suffering from serious depression over losing millions of dollars more than once. Flowing in gutsy leadership I kind of felt that the depression was always way behind me. I never intended to try to impose my faith on anyone, but it was clear to me that my Maker had reasons for allowing me to experience each bout of depression. He was bringing me closer to my leadership sweet spot and it's the only way I'd slow down and listen. When I realized that and started accepting the reality of being a highly visible leader who suffered from severe depression I learned how not to be ashamed of it. That's when I started to talk about the depression during my business conferences.

Of course at business conferences leaders who attend don't jump up and admit before the crowd that they struggle with clinical depression. I can't count how many people stand on line to speak to me at the end of my talks, or they'll email me to say they're grateful because my transparency helped them deal with their own depression. For someone who was once a legend in his own mind and took the Ten Commandments and made them "The Ten Suggestions" I now know that I'm not in charge of my ability to manage depression and continue succeeding in business. My faith and seeking the appropriate medical help assisted me in finding my God-inspired leadership moments and my business sweet spot.

Fight Off Your Personal Demons So You Can Soar

My first adult depression was in the late 1990s but up until then I was what's called a C&E Catholic because I considered myself a Christian only on Christmas and Easter. After the first depression episode I got involved with a man named Bill Wegner, who wrote the foreward in my book. Bill is one of the few full-time Catholic lay evangelists in the country who spends each year traveling around to minister, and he became a foundation and solace to me. He talked straight with me and helped me identify my own personal demons, then he helped me fight them off. Again, I was a legend in my own mind so I did arrogant things like spend thousands of dollars to take out ads in the *Sunday Asbury Park Press* so that my competitors could see the ads and get upset. I was insecure about myself so I'd do things that made me think that I looked more successful than other people who might have had more education and training than I have.

Because I didn't finish high school I suffered greatly from a lack of formal education in my early years. While many of my competitors had degrees from prestigious universities, my degree was from *Hard Knocks University*. That prevented some people from dealing with me as a credible source to be giving financial advice. Having no formal education also meant that my grammatical and English skills have always been poor, which I'm sure to some of my competitors represented another reason to mock my credibility as a reliable business advisor. At this point, I get help from literary experts before I publish anything and I find that I learn from their honest feedback. In my business dealings I try to use that same level of honesty when I deal with clients and associates, which isn't always the easiest thing to do.

Leading Based on Personal Convictions is Not Always Easy

I learned in my business that there are basically two types of advisors – those who say what they think and those who say what they think people want to hear. My world is filled with the latter.

After only a few years in the business I forecasted a stock market crash back in 1987 but the firm that I worked for wanted me to retract the forecast or resign from the company. I refused to do either and within two months the market crashed. I always wonder whether my life would be where it is had I succumbed to them and changed my statement. I stood by my decision but it's difficult to do when you find yourself being the exception and not the rule. I asked myself whether I was willing to be outspoken even if it would be perceived as me not being politically correct in an extremely politically correct industry.

Being outspoken and not hedging comes easy to me but it sometimes comes attached to trouble. I believe it's not beneficial to anyone for a leader to give someone advice and at the end of the day have the person ask, 'What exactly did the leader tell us to do?' Gutsy leaders are ones who give advice about sound decisions they've made without really knowing if their decision will be the right one in the long run.

Make Sound Decisions

People tend to believe that we have some type of crystal ball we use to make one hundred percent correct calls about every business matter. Leaders don't always know whether their decisions are the right ones or wrong ones, but gutsy leaders act on instinct despite the unknown.

I was thirty-one years old when I forecasted the stock market crash and I had been in the business for less than three years. That was when the market was 2,700 whereas now it's about 18,000. I started carefully observing the overall mood on Wall Street and the way everyone was acting and I knew in my gut that something was wrong with the market. At the time, I told myself that if the market crashed I would be a hero and if it didn't no one would really care about my forecast.

An interesting thing that I put in my book is that the day after I made the forecast, the chairman of the company I was working for called me up to New York to meet with him. I traveled there with the branch manager, who was the guy who'd previously asked me to retract my forecast or resign from the company. He said, 'Let me explain why this won't work for you. Ninety percent of the people will never sell everything like you're recommending. If your forecast is wrong, which we think it is, you'll be the laughing stock in the business world and no one will ever believe anything you say again. Let's say you're right and ninety percent of the investors don't follow your advice because they'll be so badly hurt financially that they won't be in any shape to listen to you. The ten percent who do listen to you will have about half who will be too afraid to act when you tell them to. The bottom line is that only five percent of our clients would benefit from your financial advice. Peter, you can't stay on Wall Street with only five percent.' From a sales point of view my associate made absolute sense. My gut told me otherwise even though I was probably afraid about what might happen to my future in business if I turned out to be wrong.

Fear Can Be a Reaction for Leaders

Perhaps to this day fear is still a battle of mine when it comes to some business decisions. I don't believe a person can suffer from severe depression without fear being a major component. My personal belief is that fear is as an evil that robs me of my faith. There are now times at two o'clock or three o'clock in the morning when fearful thoughts wake me up and I allow anxiety to slip in for a few minutes.

One person who helped me learn how to deal with fear as a leader is my business partner, former New York Giant, Lee Rouson. One day he said to me, 'Peter, fear is an unnatural act and is not something created for this earth. It doesn't matter whether you believe the Christian story or not. If you study the earth's creation and all the things that were put here, they were mostly put here for good and beauty. Fear is not good and it's not beautiful, therefore, it's not a natural act so don't allow an unnatural act to overcome you.' I've learned that fear is a potential reaction of mine so as a leader I remind myself that even though it's a potential reaction it's not a natural reaction. That helps me keep my game face on so that people following me don't give in to their own fears.

Keep Your Leadership Game Face On

Leaders have to do their best to keep fear under control because I believe one of the worst things that can happen is for a leader to look lost and afraid. I've never been in battle or war but I would want the person who's about to lead me into battle to avoid suddenly getting the shakes because that would make me just a little nervous about following the person. I also believe it's important that leaders understand some of the followers will be afraid and the leader should show some level of compassion as he or she helps someone overcome fear.

Lead With Compassion and Humility

In my early days I didn't understand the role of compassion in helping people overcome their fears. Twenty years ago I might have looked down on someone who was experiencing a rough time and then ask myself and others why the person let him or herself get that way. Now I wonder about what might have contributed to the person getting to a low point.

It was probably self-pride that limited me from showing empathy toward people during my early leadership days. I remember being extremely prideful and buying a house because it had a three hundred foot driveway and I wanted everybody to be impressed as they walked up the driveway.

Self-pride is arguably one of the first things leaders might need to deal with. I'm not suggesting that we shouldn't be proud of our accomplishments, but pride that's self-serving is really a form of arrogance that can easily get in the way of a leader's potential for success. Leaders might need to self-reflect to determine whether self-pride is hindering their leadership progress.

Identify What You Need to Personally Improve

I reflect a lot about what I do and how I do it and my biggest challenge right now is not wanting to use notes for presentations and interviews because I like to just speak.

The problem is I have to try to recall the specific reason I'm brought in to speak and not to go off on tangents that have nothing to do with the business topic. For instance, I recently spoke in Canada and there was a particular topic I was to cover. Somebody asked a question and I went off on a tangent and started talking about my faith. Later on one of the event coordinators said, 'Peter, we like what you do but you lost sight of what you were here for.' After that experience I started developing notes, which is a struggle for me. The real issue here is preparedness, which is something I don't believe I'm very good at and choose not to do whenever possible. I like to wing things but winging it in certain business venues is not the best thing to do.

I think if I were going around and giving my testimony in churches it might be fine for me to speak without notes and just tell my story. In business environments where people are looking for specifics and a leader has been brought in under those specifics, an audience can become disconnected if the leader tries to speak from the cuff.

As leaders it's important for us to remember the purpose of a gathering and give different audiences what they need. I had to learn that I can and should base my work on biblical principles but I can't preach to an audience if that's not what people are there for even if that's my preference.

Mr. Anthony Beshara, co-owner of New Jersey's luxurious *Bella Vista Country Club* (BVCC), resides in New Jersey with his wife, Jackie. Mr. Beshara and his cousin, Gary Beshara, who both grew up in Brooklyn, New York, partner to operate the highly successful family business in Marlboro, New Jersey. As a prestigious country club, BVCC hosts a large number of networking and charitable events each year, along with weddings, golf outings, anniversary celebrations, and private or group dining. Mr. Beshara is also a current board member of the *Monmouth County Chamber of Commerce*.

http://www.bellavistacc.com/

Anthony Beshara

Different Messages Motivate Leaders

Some things can have a profound impact on you as a gutsy leader. These things can be from real life, movies or television. For example, since I was a young kid I've loved *Star Trek*. I didn't just love *Star Trek* the television show but I loved what the show stood for. William Shatner's character, Captain Kirk, had a very strong and commanding presence. Although the show was scripted the loyalty, dedication and trust that the other characters had for Captain Kirk's power was remarkable.

There were profound messages from the show like, 'I don't believe in a no-win scenario.' One episode was about changing the computer because in order to get into the Star Fleet Academy they had to pass a test which no cadet in the history of the star fleet had ever passed. Captain Kirk fought all types of battles in re-programming the computer and some say he cheated. I believe he was creative and innovative and had the guts to think of a different way of doing something major to overcome a challenge. Traditionally, the challenge had been approached one way. Captain Kirk had the guts to try things another way. To me, this is what a gutsy leader does.

Be Brave Enough to Shift Traditions

It takes guts to shift against trends in an established industry. Take golf, for instance. As a non-golfer I see so many things in the industry that contribute to some of the challenges facing the industry as a whole. For example, the industry has isolated women for many years but now that the traditional pool of golfers is drying up the industry is trying hard to recruit women golfers because they represent a large segment of business executives.

Now the industry is waking up. Years ago creating events that would draw women into golf would have been the thing to do. A male golfer who loves golf would belong to a club but there wouldn't be anything for his wife. After a while I questioned why things were being done a certain way and I decided to be a paradigm shifter. I know I can't change the entire industry but I aim to change one person at a time during my conversations with them. By thinking long term and staying on the cutting edge regarding trends in the industry we avoided having BVCC wait until the last minute to make significant changes that helped redefine and improve our business. We were willing to risk exploring and implementing forward thinking change. Many of our competitors lacked the leadership in this area and as a result they now find themselves playing catch-up.

Stay Current with Trends

The country club industry is currently scrambling because until a few years ago social media wasn't part of the industry's conversation. I remember getting involved with social media causing BVCC to become one of the first country clubs to navigate those waters. Facebook wasn't where we engaged in idle chatter. We decided it would be where we'd do targeted marketing and promotions to help grow our business. Not having a massive marketing budget meant we had to find alternative and innovative ways to attract people to BVCC in order to grow revenue in an industry that was changing very rapidly and leaving behind many victims of indecision.

Coach People to Protect the Brand

Getting your staff on the same page to protect the brand can be a challenge at times. You can have staff members who are very loyal but are not always the best brand ambassadors. For example, have you ever gone to a restaurant, sat down, ordered your meal, and as you're about to take the first bite of food the waiter or waitress will come over and say, 'How is everything?' Think of the logic behind that question. The customer's mouth is full of food and the employee takes that exact moment to ask, 'How are things?' We can ruin a customer's experience by mishandling the small details.

I often wondered what would happen if the customer swallowed and said things were not going well during his or her dining experience. That conversation would lead to a great discussion about the importance of everyone on the team protecting the brand. Coaching teams to protect every aspect of the brand requires training, re-training, and more training.

Build Human Capital

Building human capital can be one of the biggest challenges a leader has to face. Your staff might be loyal, dedicated and good people but their skill sets might need retuning to match the needs of the organization. This has been a leadership challenge for me over the years. We need people who we know will support and defend the brand. The difficulty comes in having individuals on staff that haven't performed their jobs well even after a lot of training. Leaders have to always discover and pursue the path that in the end is the best for the success of the organization.

As leaders we have to weigh the variables when we closely examine the work of each individual staff member. I don't believe there's really a one-size-fits-all model for building human capital in an organization since every staff member's needs might be vastly different from the rest. That's not to say we don't provide whole-staff training and development because we have to. However, during training sessions I'm closely monitoring who seems to be getting it and who seems to need custom-tailored instructions.

The Training Doesn't Stop

We believe that if you were hired to be part of BVCC you must have had some qualities during the interview process that made us believe you would fit in well here. Once we bring people on board we have a responsibility to build their capacity. Staff training never stops here, sometimes for what I consider silly things. For example, there might be a bartender who is very relational and engaging with the customers, which is what we want and need in a thriving country club business. But, that same person might work behind the bar for an eight-hour shift and never notice one of the overhead lights has been off the entire time, making it difficult for our valued customers to see what they're drinking or eating.

In that instance the training we provide might be two-fold: one-on-one for that particular bartender with specific feedback about engaging customers in a well-lit environment, and whole-staff with general tips about the importance of being aware of their surroundings in a client-oriented business.

I'd rather remain proactive regarding staff training versus feeling as if I stand at the front door of BVCC wearing a tuxedo and welcome guests into the establishment, while our staff members stand in the dining hall and usher guests out of the back door because they don't know how to provide the quality service BVCC is known for. As I mentioned earlier, leaders have to constantly make sure the people being led remain on the same vision page the leader is one from year to year, and dare I say, from day to day.

Keep Everyone on One Vision Page

I've found that regardless of how many staff meetings or training sessions a leader conducts, or how the leader tries to project him or herself as a coach, mentor or friend; there are times when staff members just don't seem to be on the same page the leader is on. Moving people onto the same vision page for the betterment of the organization is critical. As leaders we have to help staff members identify whether they're not on the same page as the leader because they don't know, they're afraid, or they're unwilling to be there. That identification gives the leader useful information about who should be on the team and who might need to look for a different team.

Mr. Clifford Moore is the owner of *Kazia's Asian Grab 'n Go* on Route 36 in Keyport, New Jersey, and he is the former owner of the famous IHOP Restaurant on Route 36 in Keyport. *"I am an entrepreneur who has owned several small businesses in Monmouth County, New Jersey. My companies include: Kazia's Asian Grab 'n Go – Keyport, New Jersey, IHOP Restaurant - Keyport, New Jersey, MOORE YARN at Airport Plaza - Hazlet, New Jersey, The Belly Flop Cafe - Hazlet, New Jersey, I'm Impressed, Inc - Public Speaking and Professional Facilitator, The Brand of ME - Personal Development Workshops & Coaching, The Social Media Wizards - Social Media Outsourcing, Valued Connections.BIZ - an online directory that connects businesses with businesses and customers to those businesses. I am a Networker who values and shares information and referrals with over 72,000+ followers on Twitter, 2,700+ Facebook Friends, 5,700+ Likes on Business Page, 2,300+ connections on LinkedIn, 999+ Friends on FourSquare."* In addition, Mr. Moore provides professional training and coaching throughout New Jersey. He currently fills the role of Commissioner with the Monmouth County Board of Taxation at The State of New Jersey. In the past, Mr. Moore served as Partner at Community Publications & MarketME Printing, Owner of the Neptune, New Jersey

IHOP Restaurant, Manager of Ops Services and Operations Consultant for IHOP Restaurants, Managing Partner of Boston Market, Vice President of Operations at Byers Restaurants, Regional Vice President of Sbarro, The Italian Eatery, and F & B Auditor at Beefsteak Charlie's. He is the President Emeritus of the Northern Monmouth Chamber of Commerce and continues to serve on the Executive Board of the chamber, which is now the Monmouth County Chamber of Commerce (MCCC). As President of the Business Improvement District in Keyport, New Jersey, Mr. Moore works with the board to assess the needs of the different members of the community, and then develop plans of action that best utilize the resources that are available for the benefit of the entire community. He also serves as the Co-Chair of the Hazlet Business Owners Association's Economic Development Committee, President of the Keyport Bayfront Business Cooperative (Keyport BID), and Board Member of the Bayshore Senior Center. The committee was charged with attracting new businesses to the two highway corridors of Route 35 and Route 36, and then supporting the business efforts throughout the area. *"Serving on the Board of the New Jersey Conference and Visitors Bureau allows me the opportunity to get the much needed support in marketing and advertising in the Bayshore Area."* Mr. Moore's honors and awards include: Army Commendation Medal 1978; IHOP Operations Consultant of the Year 2001;

Northern Monmouth Chamber 2009 President's Award; Keyport Mayor's Certificate of Recognition 2009; Paul Harris Fellowship Award 2011; President of the Northern Monmouth Chamber 2011-2013; Official Medal from the Mayor and Township Committee of Hazlet December 2012; Distinguished Service Citation from the Mayor and Township Committee of Hazlet December 2012; New Jersey Restaurant Association Good Samaritan Award 2013; Certificate of Special Congressional Recognition by Congressman Frank Pallone, Jr.; Recognition/Proclamation Certificate by the Monmouth County Board of Chosen Freeholders; Assembly Resolution by the New Jersey General Assembly; Community Service Award by the Community Affairs & Resource Center; Boy Scouts of America - Twin Lights District "Hometown Hero Award" April 2013, and the Declaration of "Cliff Moore Day" in Monmouth County on March 28, 2014. Mr. Moore's accomplishments also include Organizer of the Northern Monmouth Chamber of Commerce Beacon of Hope Disaster & Humanitarian Relief after Superstorm Sandy (officially known as "Hurricane Sandy"). Mr. Moore graduated from St. Mary's College Preparatory School in Rutherford, New Jersey, and attended Central Texas College. "I am always looking to make things more efficient and cost effective. Developing people to be the best they can be." Mr. Moore's specialty areas include Publishing, Training, Testing, Communications, Public Speaking, Certified Compass Coach, Management Workshop

Facilitator, and Social Media Activist. His membership includes Hazlet's Land Use Board Member; President of Hazlet's Recreation Commission Keyport Business Improvement District; Member of the Matawan-Aberdeen Rotary Club; Member of the Monmouth-Ocean Development Council; Member of the Hazlet Business Owners Association; Co-Chair of the HBOA Economic Development Committee; Member of the New Jersey Restaurant Association , National Restaurant Association, NY/NJ IHOP Steering Committee; Former Board Member of the Jersey Shore Convention & Visitors Bureau, and Board Member of the Bayshore Area Senior Health, Education and Recreation Center. Mr. Moore and his wife, Mitzi, live in New Jersey with their two children.

Ms. Mitzi Moore is the Founder & Owner of *Moore Yarn* located in the Airport Plaza in Hazlet, New Jersey. With the business tag, *"We'll keep you in stitches,"* Moore Yarn is committed to the *knitters and hookers* – people who knit and crochet – of the New Jersey Bayshore Area. The business sells yarn, supplies, books, and patterns. Ms. Moore says, *"With over 1,300 different yarns and colors to choose from, Moore Yarn provides a comfortable and relaxing place to hang out to knit and crochet. We want to become your Yarn Hangout! We do not stock the same yarn as other craft shops do. Come in and make yourself comfortable and knit or crochet with like-minded people at any time."* Moore Yarn does not require visitors to purchase supplies or materials and provides free patterns, coaching, coffee and "knibbles." They even allow visitors to bring in their problems or questions about projects they are working on so that one of Moore Yarn's experts can assist them at no charge (https://www.mooreyarn.com). Ms. Moore is married to Mr. Cliff Moore, and they have a son and a daughter. They were instrumental in helping to revitalize the Bayshore Area business community after it was devastatingly struck by Superstorm Sandy (officially known as "Hurricane Sandy") in October 2012.

Cliff & Mitzi Moore

Go With Your Gut after Being Burned

Gutsy leadership is revealed when you get experience or have exposure through accomplishments in business, education or other areas. You know you'll get burned a couple of times but courage and vision help you continue jumping in without fear even after you've been burned. When leaders are specific about what they need and where they're going there's less of a likelihood for them to get burned so easily by people.

Be Specific With the Team about What You Need

The *Beacon of Hope* is as an example of us being very specific about our leadership needs and then having people come through in all areas. The *Beacon of Hope* happened within twenty-four hours after Superstorm Sandy hit New Jersey in October of 2012. The experience took us from having twenty donation tables to having a distribution center that took care of a hundred thousand people within three weeks.

One of the things I believe is a strength of mine is identifying good key people and putting together the right team. I do that by communicating the vision and then letting team members be the experts in different areas.

Father Dan, a local priest, knew the community and immediately set up the *Beacon of Hope* through the church. He set up twenty donation tables because the thought was that everything would be back to normal after about three days. We learned quickly that we'd need a plan that included having tractor trailers come from all over to deliver huge amounts of items to be distributed for large amounts of people who were impacted by the storm.

We didn't know anything about large distributions or storing the items so I called individuals who did. The Northern Monmouth Chamber of Commerce (now called the Monmouth County Chamber of Commerce) also got involved and arranged for a local bus company to send buses to areas where people couldn't get out of their homes to come and get items. We were specific with the team about what we needed and everyone did his or her part. Of course we had to adjust the plan as we went along as we ran into obstacles.

Adjust the Plan to Keep the Purpose on Track

When just twenty tables were used for the distribution efforts things got a little chaotic at times because there were so many people who needed help but there wasn't a big enough system in place yet. We suggested identifying which of the four hundred volunteers would be responsible for different areas and made anyone in a red vest a decision maker, and anyone in a yellow vest a specialist. If people needed to know where to store an item they asked a specialist. If they needed a decision made they went to a person in a red vest. We held daily orientations and trainings so the volunteers continued to feel a part of the purpose of what we were actually doing to restore hope to entire communities. Our volunteers kept the effort working.

Volunteer Whenever You Can

Even as leaders we volunteer for anything we can volunteer for and we give to anybody we can give to. We don't call it paying things forward because we're not looking for anything in return. We volunteer for the good of the whole community. For example, when I was working in the *Beacon of Hope* I'd usually be there from eight o'clock in the morning until ten or eleven o'clock at night. Mitzi was still running our business and we had lost power for a while in our own home. In addition to running the business, she and our kids volunteered at the middle school which had been converted into a temporary shelter for seniors. We've always just accepted our leadership roles and moved forward in them.

Accept Your Leadership Mantle

I don't think I've ever been part of an organization or a group where I haven't ended up assuming a leadership role.

I've been on a county board for a short while now and made some recommendation that were implemented. Because I'm the outsider I'm comfortable making suggestions about areas I believe need improvement. I mention that we own several businesses to establish the fact that we've got credibility right out of the box and I have experience successfully managing business initiatives.

Leaders have to be comfortable accepting leadership mantles when their credibility not only gets them a seat at the table, but gets them audience with individuals and organizations that can influence change.

Leadership Can Start During Youth So Identify Skill Sets

I'm the oldest of five children. I've got three brothers and a sister. In the neighborhood we lived in there were about four other houses in the area that all had five children within the same age group. It always seemed that when there was a problem everyone would come to me to help find a solution. They knew that if I didn't know the answer I would research until I discovered it. A lot of times it was up to me to help everyone else see the possibility of overcoming challenges and believe that we could do whatever we put our minds to.

Be Open to What's Next

The word *can't* is not in my vocabulary and if someone says they can't do something I ask, 'Why can't you do it? What stops you from doing it? How can I help you do what you need to do?'

For instance, I tell my employees in every one of our businesses that when they have to do something it's my job to help eliminate any obstacles or barriers preventing them from getting their jobs done well. Granted, some hurdles are tougher than others to overcome but it's up to me as the leader to do all that I can to help people change their perspectives so they see barriers as opportunities for growth. I'm constantly thinking of ways to help people open up to leadership opportunities that might be next for them.

I have no idea what's next on the horizon for us. We just opened our eighth business during the fall, which is an Asian cuisine restaurant in the Airport Plaza in Hazlet, New Jersey. People ask me if I want to run for a higher political office but I don't know yet. If that happens it happens and if it doesn't, it doesn't. We believe there will always be some new leadership opportunity waiting for us to grab hold of. We stay open to what's next.

Mr. Victor Scudiery a Newark, New Jersey native, earned a degree in Business Administration from Seton Hall University in 1956. He was inducted into the Seton Hall Stillman School of Business Entrepreneurial Hall of Fame in 2011. While living in Newark, Mr. Scudiery was active in local politics, campaigning hard to ensure that Democrats were elected to office. He served in the U.S. Army for two years in Active Military Duty and for four years on Reserve Duty. Mr. Scudiery moved to Monmouth County, New Jersey in 1968. He is the owner and operator of several businesses, including Interstate Electronics, Inc. (IEI). The successfully operating IEI opened its doors in 1978 and the company currently occupies 40,000 square feet of space at the Airport Plaza Shopping Center in Hazlet, New Jersey, which Mr. Scudiery also owns. His experience in communications and media led him to produce books, albums and television shows seen across the United States and Europe. Two of his award-winning productions include *Face to Face with Jacki Walker,* a weekly talk show that addressed issues pertinent to New Jersey, and *The Murder of Maria Marshall.* Mr. Scudiery also established and served as chairman of a non-profit radio station that transmitted from Airport Plaza. *"Successful business people should be involved in social issues."* That thought has led Mr.

Scudiery to be a generous benefactor and philanthropist who sits on the boards of a number of local civic organizations. He is a former member of the Brookdale College Learning Center Advisory Board, and he is currently the Chairman and Trustee of the Bayshore Senior Health, Education and Recreation Center. Mr. Scudiery is regarded as an asset and community leader in the Bayshore Area because of his high level of business integrity and ongoing philanthropic and humanitarian efforts to promote the success of businesses in the Bayshore Area and throughout New Jersey. Mr. Scudiery has also been recognized for his service and dedication during his tenure as Chairman of the Bayshore Health Care Center Board of Trustees, the Buck Smith Scholarship Award Foundation, and the Board of Directors for the Bayshore Community Hospital and Bayshore Community Health Services. He was recognized and awarded for his hard work, generosity and compassion with the Bayshore Community Hospital Humanitarian of the Year Award in 2006. Mr. Scuidery also received the YMCA Citizen Service Award in 2010. In addition, he served under former Governor Brendon Byrne on the Ethic Advisory Council, as Co-Chairman of the Boy Scouts of Monmouth County, as Chairman of the Hazlet Economic Development Group, as Co-Chairman of the Bayshore Economic Development Program, as Technical Advisor at Kean College, as Associate Director of the United Jersey Bank, and on the Brookdale College Learning Center Advisory Board. Mr. Scudiery also held the position of Chairman of the Monmouth County Democratic party from 1989 to 2012 when he retired from the post. He is the publisher of *The Papal Review*, a pictorial essay of each Catholic Pope since Saint Peter. Mr. Scudiery produced and directed a commemorative album of Pope John Paul II, and a series of children's educational albums and coloring books. He helped set the trend of exercising to music with the first series of *Dancercise* albums. Mr. Scudiery currently lives in the Bayshore Area and serves as an honorary board member of the Monmouth County Chamber of Commerce. He enjoys spending time with his significant other, Margaret, and with family and close friends, especially his daughter Viki, who was a successful international fashion model and as a graduate of the Brennan School of Healing is currently an Energy Medicine Practitioner.

Mr. Victor Scudiery

Take the Bull by the Horns

Gutsy leaders take the bull by the horns and just move forward. Many times I attend meetings and different people suggest what to do but they won't offer to be part of getting things done. You wind up taking the bull by its horns and getting things done. I think gutsy leaders acknowledge that early on in their careers and they become comfortable with it.

Know Your Leadership Direction Early On

I believe that I knew the direction I was going in at a very young age. My father owned a small dry cleaning business in Newark on South Orange Avenue and I decided to sell toys out of the store's front window. When I was fifteen or sixteen I would have someone drive me to Canal Street in New York to buy toys and jewelry at wholesale prices and then sell them out of my father's business. Then, I opened a jack rabbit valet service to pick up and drop the dry cleaned items. Someone with a driver's license would drive me to pick up and drop off clothes to and from the shop. Those are business ventures that were successful but I had my share of failures.

Chart Your Own Success Despite Failed Attempts

Not all of my business ventures were successful. For example, I owned a tavern in Irvington originally called Carousel (later called The Tiffany Lounge). That business didn't do well. Neither did Sub Haven in Linden or Gaiters Restaurant in Sea Bright. I decided to move on from those failures and learn from any business mistakes I'd made. This is a true sign of a gutsy leader. While others commiserate failures, we use them as a proven foundation to build upon.

I bought the Airport Shopping Plaza in Hazlet in 1978 and opened an electronics store in one of its retail locations. The plaza was very depressed when I bought it but today it's a thriving retail location in the Bayshore Area. My electronics store remains one of the successful businesses in the plaza. I've always believed that in order to be successful the people around you must also be successful. With that, I pulled together business owners and executives from the Monmouth County Chamber of Commerce (formerly known as the Northern Monmouth Chamber of Commerce) and invited them to hold their business meetings in my executive board room in the plaza. My work with the senior center over a twenty-five year period was another way to bring business vibrancy back to the area. Today, several other organizations hold their business meetings in our executive board room. Huge leadership moments just seemed to make themselves available to me and I pursued every one of them.

The Moments Just Started Happening

I really don't know how I knew when it was my moment to lead. All I know is that I wanted to get businesses to relocate to Airport Plaza and along the highway. To me, the purpose was to draw more commerce to the area and that kept me going despite my previous failed business ventures.

I moved my electronics store here and that was a good thing. I was convinced that I didn't want big chain stores here because I felt that if one big chain closed there would be problems for all of the other businesses in the plaza. So, I pursued small businesses to trust the plaza with their businesses by dividing up the plaza from one section to the other.

Including the Motor Vehicle Commission, we've got small businesses throughout the plaza and we're fully occupied. I always want as many tenants as possible, which adds more employees to patronize all of our businesses. I think that's probably led to the success of the Airport Plaza businesses. We support each other's success. I didn't know how successful we would be when I first got here because things didn't look that great around us.

You Might Have to Journey Without All the Details

It's ironic that I purchased the Airport Plaza before actually seeing it. When I did finally see what I'd invested in I was literally afraid but I told myself that I'd gotten into a hole that only success would get me out of. I hung in there and made it work even without having all of the details at the start. I think the reality of being afraid about what I saw as a potential business fiasco motivated me to press on.

Get People on the Bandwagon Even When You're Afraid

From day one fear has been a motivator for me. Stepping in the direction of the unknown actually gives me courage as a leader to move forward even though I might not know if things will work out or not. My business sense kicked in and reminded me that if there's an Airport Plaza and all of the stores are leaving something needed to be done to get businesses to stay. Then, I took immediate and strategic actions to make that happen.

There were around eight or nine stores still here when I bought the plaza. There was an absentee Laundromat that had broken front windows. This is the kind of thing potential business owners would see when they came to the area and exited the Garden State Parkway before making a quick U-turn. The environment was depressed and I said to myself, 'You have to make this area look presentable so businesses want to move back.' Before I knew it other people jumped on the bandwagon and said, 'Well, if Vic is working on it and it looks like it's improving, let's do the same thing.'

Lay the Foundation for People Who'll Lead After You

The senior center was in horrible shape. I was on that board for about thirty years and there were a lot of politicians on the board. I wasn't a senior when I first joined the board but I would always ask, 'Why would a senior want to be here as depressed looking as it is?' We started revitalizing the first floor and we also put a second floor in. Now, the place is flourishing and it's unbelievable to see the amount of people we currently serve. We also put a healthcare center in there and that turned out to be a magnificent move. Before each new development I would always ask, 'Why would I want to come here if I were a senior citizen?'

It took many years to complete the senior center project but I wouldn't give up on it. I think it has the basic foundation to continue thriving. Every month I would worry about whether we could pay the rent or not. We were constantly in the red each year and we'd have to fundraise to stay afloat. Within the past two years we've had money coming in since we regularly rent out the banquet hall. It was important to me to establish a system that worked well so that anyone taking over after I retire will have the foundation laid out.

Your Foundation Gives Perspective

Deep down inside I suppose I kept leading because of my upbringing. I grew up in a very poor neighborhood and we didn't own a television or any of the modern conveniences. Growing up that way can cause a leader to see why he or she wants to pursue success and to have the strength to fight giants along the way.

You Will Have to Fight Giants

Revitalizing this area was challenging and scary. After I visited the shopping center and saw dirt floors and a lot of stores in the mall that were never finished I questioned myself about what I'd invested in. The town charged me fines because kids would hang out on the dirt floors and litter the area surrounding the vacant storefronts.

I relocated my electronics store to the other end of the mall and remember getting fined for something. That's when I decided to get involved in local politics. When I first took over the shopping center and wanted to divide the stores the town told me I could not do just about everything I wanted to do. I thought the town was wrong and should've helped me because the whole area was depressed and my projects were trying to help change that.

I never built anything without getting the proper permits or going before the planning board or the zoning board. Consistently doing the right thing and staying current about what was happening with other business organizations outside of the area helped me act on ideas I had about restoring this business community.

Be More Than an Idea Generator – Act on Ideas

There are a lot of leaders who come up with ideas but they don't pursue them. The biggest thing is pursuing the ideas even if they might not work out the way you expect. You might have to go backwards sometimes in order to move forward again but gutsy leaders just don't give up.

I've been in so many businesses, some successes and some failures. I've been in the record business and I wrote the Papal Review, which is a short history of all the Popes and St. Peter. I developed building kits and put together cassette recordings explaining the background about what was being built. Radio Shack sold the kits. I put out the first exercising record called *Dancercise with Solid Gold*. I put out some records with Lionel Hampton and Buddy Rich. I switched business lanes whenever the opportunities presented themselves.

Switch Lanes When You Need To

The electronics business was my main business and although it's not at all a glamorous business, it is a successful business and served to feed any previous business failures. When I went into the record industry I was looking for something more glamorous. Even opening a restaurant was a pursuit of glamour.

The record business was successful, especially the jazz series with Lionel Hampton. It was more successful in Japan because Japan had been looking for jazz for a long time so our sales were successful there. When my partner in the record industry passed away I backed away from that business. My partner was good at it and had saved some of the specialty albums I'd put together. They were commemorative albums like the John Paul II album, which gained momentum worldwide. I then put out coloring books with audio cassettes for kids. I changed a story like *The Three Little Pigs* and described the clothes they wore. Kids could color along while listening to the story being read aloud. That also worked out very well. There always seemed to be something on the horizon, which is what people came to expect from me.

Gutsy Leading is a Natural Thing

I've enjoyed this interview so much because leading is just a natural thing for me. I knew I couldn't let a few failures prevent me from moving forward and I thought hard about what I failed at and why. Then I set out to make sure it didn't happen again. Just by being gutsy in my leadership has paid off for a lot more people than just me. That's made it all worth it.

IT TAKES GUTS

In response to our question about what the term *gutsy transformational leader* means, our leaders confirmed our hypothesis that gutsy leadership really is in some people's DNA!

Here are some of the trends and common themes that emerged from the responses.

Gutsy leaders:

- Make mistakes but keep moving forward.
- Accept being wrong.
- Sometimes have fear and anxiety, however, cling to fearlessness, boldness and courage.
- Stay current, relevant and adaptable.
- Expect giant challenges to confront and see them as opportunities.
- Are used to having people vacillate between loving them and hating them, and including them and isolating them.
- Are authentic, humble, consistent and trustworthy.
- Know whose needs are being met.
- Get results.
- Strategically pursue excellence and success.
- Are coachable and listen to a trusted advisory team.
- Ask the tough questions.

- Are tradition shifters when necessary.
- Are reflective thinkers and learners.
- Are clear and specific about purpose, strengths, needs and brand.
- Can work through uncertainty without melting.
- Do what's right.
- Build upon human capital so systems can be built.
- Are comfortable being radically different.
- Connect with the right people.
- Focus on assembling the best team to do the work.
- Are responsive not reactionary.
- Are networkers and political strategists.
- Are eager to re-invent themselves.
- Are legacy builders with stories to share.
- Have the guts to embrace their individual leadership wiring and calling.
- Believe the word *can't* is not in the vocabulary...

We used a popular social media platform and asked leaders to weigh in on a question. Here is the question and the unfiltered responses we got:

In one word, what keeps leaders moving forward despite barriers and challenges?

1 response	2 responses	3 responses	4 responses
Resilience	Persistence	Vision	Faith/Believing/Believe
Discipline	Grit		
Hope	Commitment		
Creativity	Children/Students		
Information			
Target			
Culture			
Comfort			
Adaptation			
Purpose			
Mortgage			
Skill			
Megalomania			
Sex Appeal			
Compassion			
Optimism			
Love			

OUR THOUGHTS

"Practice makes permanent, not perfect."
—Dr. Sharon M. Biggs (circa 2003)

Dr. Sharon M. Biggs

It's Nothing Personal. It's Just Business.

What do gutsy transformational leaders do when they have plans in place to accomplish a vision and mission and then life happens? *They keep on tickin' while they take a lickin'!* Gutsy leaders who lead from the front take deep breaths and remind themselves that regarding everything, *it's nothing personal...it's just business.*

Take Deep Breaths

Leading from the front means I oftentimes don't have the luxury of pausing to breathe when I'm in the thick of a leadership moment. I just have to take deep breaths while I stay laser-focused on moving people, organizations and goals forward. This reality sometimes makes it difficult for me to pause and slow down, but I'm a strong proponent of every leader carving out time each day for some type of *Lunch Namaste* to help clear our heads and our hearts (BIGGS-isms, 2013). I believe we either pay now with a small amount of time taken out of our schedules or we pay later with a huge amount of burnout before we get to successfully complete our moments. I've found that scheduling in daily Namaste time keeps me focused, reflective and at the top of my leadership game.

Deep Messages Penetrate Hearts and Minds of Followers

As leaders successfully complete giant leadership moments our deep breaths tend to resonate in the voices, language and actions of the people we're leading whether they publicly admit it or not.

That has been one of the most rewarding parts of my leadership journey. At times I find myself having to hold back big cheesy grins when someone I'm leading articulates words and thoughts or demonstrates actions I've coached them on. I get really excited as a leader when they speak as if they'd thought of the ideas or actions themselves! While typical leaders might get turned off when someone "steals" their ideas, it's during those times I know I've seized my giant leadership moments and helped a member of the team move up a rung or two on the leadership capacity ladder.

I experienced this as a leadership coach for school principals of failing and low-performing schools. The concept of leadership coaches for the principals was a new one, and I was one of four people in the region selected at the time to fill the role. There were enough skeptics around who seemed to want to fail the leadership coaching model before it even got off the ground. Since I was from outside of the local area I wasn't embedded or entrenched in the political fiber of the area, which allowed me to lead and coach wearing what I call *data lenses*.

Some of the school principals and their teams welcomed the leadership coaching model because they'd longed for someone to come in and help them become better leaders. Others were resistant to the changes regarding how things were being done and they were vocal about it. Since I firmly believe that data sets are a leader's best friend I kept my best friend with me at all times.

As I led the leaders in conversations about data sets I would always ask them to 'Show me the evidence to support what you've just told me because we both know opinions don't matter when we're building or re-structuring systems. And, always use talking points when you're explaining your data to me so that you don't go off on verbal tangents. I'm your leadership coach but there will be others you might need to explain your data to so you might as well practice on me.'

After about a full year the school leaders had become used to my data-focused leadership and coaching style and I'd see and hear evidence of this when I sat as an observer while they explained their data sets to other individuals or groups. So much so that if I'd closed my eyes I might have thought I was speaking and explaining the data! I still see some of those school leaders at times and they, verbatim, say what I used to say to them about showing evidence to support what's said and using talking points to stay on track.

We Stay on Track Even When We're Tired

I've also found it's particularly helpful to keep everyone's focus on moving forward versus on how fatigued the team might be. Since a gutsy leader's voice is typically the first one that is heard, it's important that a picture of unwavering strength and openness to dialogue be demonstrated by the leader.

Some might say this is a suggestion that as leaders we should be inauthentic about any obstacles or struggles but that's not at all the message here.

Gutsy leaders simply have to use extreme caution about making their personal exhaustion or frustration public because the leader's persona is contagious. A visibly exhausted, grumpy, gossipy and malcontented leader can lead to the birth of visibly exhausted, grumpy, gossipy and malcontented followers. If our followers are going to catch anything from us we want it to be unwavering strength and perseverance versus defeated weakness and a desire to quit. As leaders we need to consistently exude the message that quitting is not an option.

What Does It All Mean in the Moment?

I thought back to when I might have started walking in

my leadership calling and I remembered a third grade experience. My teacher called me to her desk one day and asked me if I would consider assisting her at Parent/Teacher Conference Night by organizing student folders containing their work, greeting parents, and then directing parents to meet with the teacher when it was their time to conference.

I thought nothing of the experience at the time because I loved my teacher and would have helped her in any way I could. When I first became involved in leadership training an activity called for that recollection and I started connecting the dots. It must have been pretty gutsy for me to tell my third grade classmates I'd been actively recruited by the teacher we shared in order to interact with their parents during what was at that time one of the most nerve-racking times in the life of any student.

At that moment I thought I was just being a good and obedient kid. In reality, my teacher was coaching me into my leadership calling. The conference night was a success and all of the parents congratulated my teacher on having such an able and professional little assistant. Ironically, my teacher spent very little time explaining to me what had to be done. I just did what I thought needed to be done and it worked. At that young age I'd already started practicing what I now call *owning the moment.*

We Do What We Believe Needs to Be Done

Even during my third grade leadership experience I simply did what I thought should be done. There was no manual. Although I was nervous I remember thinking to myself, 'What would my friends in class want me to do to get their parents ready for either a positive report from the teacher or a negative one?' My siblings helped me find just the right dressy outfit to wear, I put on my game face, and I tackled my leadership responsibility with confidence. Unbeknownst to me I was engaged in what I now clearly see was the use of strategic leadership to overcome a challenge. I thought the biggest challenge that conference night would be me staying up way past my bedtime in order to help my teacher. If only all of a leader's challenges were that simple and required such simplistic strategy.

Strategic Leadership Helps Overcome Challenges

Leadership challenges are always a part of every leader's current reality and I'm no different. Perhaps one of the biggest challenges for me is getting people to adapt to new and different perspectives and mindsets about how things should be done on a team, in an organization, or within a system.

When I interviewed high-performing school district superintendents for my doctoral dissertation about potential barriers to change, the number one response was the barrier of traditional and outdated mindsets of people connected to an organization. There was a lot of discussion about having to be strategic in leading people through mindset shifts that would result in behavioral changes.

Much of my leadership training has led me to rely on strategically coaching versus coercing people to make these shifts. But, my eyes were opened to one important truth: *Before I became a leadership coach I believed everyone was coachable. After I became a leadership coach I saw there might be some people who are not necessarily coachable and who need to be managed and directed more often than coached and led.*

When people being led resist, refuse and reproach every suggestion to move forward this can be frustrating for any gutsy leader who operates from a standpoint of shifting paradigms in order to change and improve systems.

Typical leaders might give in and allow resistant mindsets to stay active and determine what gets done when and by whom. *As gutsy leaders* we find innovate ways to work around, over, under and above resistant mindsets so that necessary changes and improvements can still be made. Since different gutsy leaders have different leadership brands it's important to discover the brand that fuels this level and kind of shifting.

Lead While You Find Your Brand

As gutsy leaders we might have to give this thing a few gutsy tries before we find the brand with our name on it.

Once we find our brand we become empowered and there's no limit to what we can do when we assemble the right team.

For me as a gutsy leader, I understand that I've been gifted certain default talents such as coaching, leading, teaching, mentoring and encouraging, which I'm branded to naturally tap into when I'm assigned to lead. When I see that a person or team I'm leading doesn't respond to my natural leadership skill sets I then shift to a more managerial leadership style that includes monitoring of behaviors and actions. Managerial and operational-focused leadership is awkward for me and I use those approaches only when absolutely necessary.

I also make sure I continually hone skills that enable me to carry out my leadership assignments so I'm always focused on becoming better at things such as public speaking, presenting, organizing, researching, using data and taking strategic actions. Those skill sets are helpful whether I'm coaching or managing individuals and teams.

Purposeful Leadership Assignments

I've discovered that I've been most impactful when I've identified and acknowledged the purpose of a given leadership assignment. As leaders we have to recognize that purpose might change as leadership assignments change. This is by far a leadership lesson that has deeply resonated in my gut as a result of my varied leadership assignments and years of leadership training and development at the graduate and doctoral levels.

Some researchers refer to this as adaptive leadership while others say it's leadership that's situational. I believe that regardless of the leadership label, gutsy leaders must be ready and willing to switch up and use different leadership, coaching, consulting and managerial approaches as problems being solved call for it.

The leadership approaches might need to vary from organization to organization, from team to team, from person to person, and from day to day. The capacity level and openness of the people being led generally determines which approach I've needed to use at any given moment.

It takes guts to lead this way because switching approaches might sometimes be interpreted by observers as indecisiveness or an inability to address leadership issues the same way any of the observers might address the issues. In reality, for gutsy leaders each action and step is strategically developed, determined and executed. I believe that the bigger the leadership issue the bigger the opportunity to seize a true leadership moment and that motivates me.

As a gutsy leader I've had to become comfortable with being misunderstood, misjudged, misrepresented and even disliked during giant leadership moments. It's during those times that I've already mentally mapped out what a successful end result might look like. I'm aware that it wouldn't be wise or prudent to share all of the details about the journey with either the people I'm leading or with the outside observers because they'll generally want to add their opinions and two cents to the mix. During those times I'm not looking for people's opinions because I'm relying on data sets to drive my actions. To me, external opinions risk cluttering data that I use to drive my leadership decisions.

I'm very self-reflective about my leadership but I've found that I've had to learn how to evict, eliminate, reduce, and sometimes ignore external chatter from people about what might have gone wrong with an initial leadership approach I've used. I remind myself that not every leadership approach will work well with everyone the first time around and that there's a lot of research to support that truth.

I leave space for my consistent actions to let people I'm leading and people observing my leadership see this truth come to light. I've found that time, space and consistency tends to outweigh external opinions.

As leaders we have to not only be adaptable and flexible in our leadership approaches, but we have to be forgiving of ourselves when things don't go right the first time around. Remember, we might have to give this thing a few good college tries before we discover the brand that works in each leadership moment.

Gutsy leaders actually find this more exciting and empowering than frustrating and we own opportunities to confront failed attempts and turn them into giant leadership moments!

Empower Others As You Become More Empowered |

I'm convinced we can avoid experiencing a leadership vacuum if we continue focusing on empowering other leaders to answer their leadership callings.

As a woman leader I reflect a lot about what I might be able to do to help coach aspiring and practicing leaders, just as my third grade teacher did for me.

Writing is a form of *Namaste Time* for me as a leader since I believe I was born to write and make stories come to life through the written word. I recently wrote a blog article (see below) about what I believe women in leadership can do to help other women tap into their untapped leadership capacities and abilities. There's no convoluted formula. Simply put, it's empowerment.

Empowered Women Leaders Empower Other Women

I appreciate the magnitude of Women's History Month every March and tried to decide how I could best celebrate women leaders this year. In thinking about women in leadership I've come to one conclusion based on my own professional and personal observations:

Empowered women leaders empower other women while weakened women leaders weaken other women.

A number of leadership books remind leaders to be self-reflective and adaptive in their leadership. As we, the Sisterhood of Leadership, reflect this month about how we lead let's simply ask ourselves which category we currently exist in – the empowered group or the weakened group.

If we're empowered let's continue re-defining ourselves so we become even more empowered. If we're weakened let's find an empowered woman leader we trust who can show us how to model her leadership power.

(March 2015)

"Relentless persistence is like kryptonite to bureaucracy."
—T. Biggs II (June 23, 2014)

Coach Terence H. Biggs II
Excellence Without Excuse^SM

My personal quote for many years now is, *Excellence without Excuse^SM* because I am a results-driven digital nomad with a passion for disturbing the apple cart. The excuse of *it has not been done before* just does not sit well with me. Armed with hands-on corporate experience and operating or consulting several small businesses, I approach the *dynamics of marketplace entrepreneurship* differently from many of my peers. My experiences help me when I coach and mentor other business owners and executives using my guiding business principles of honesty, integrity and fairness.

I hear from clients that before making major decisions that can impact their businesses, they come to me because they trust my business experience and judgment...I've been *fire-tested*.

Some people look at me and think that I always know the right thing to say and do in all my business dealings. The reality is that there are times when I am not sure what moves to make but I make a withdrawal from the reservoir of my past experiences (good and bad), hold myself to a very high standard of excellence, and just dive in to get things done. Sometimes both of my knees are trembling but my game face is always on. I like the saying, "never let them see you sweat." In order to do that though, you need a *well of experience* you can draw from.

I've been fortunate enough to have served in a number of leadership roles and capacities in the corporate, small business and non-profit arena for over thirty years as an Entrepreneur, Solo-preneur, Marketing & Sales Development Executive, President & CEO, Wall Street Financial Executive, Business Founder, Philanthropist, Board Member, Product Developer, International Trade Delegation Executive, Former Retail Store Owner & Operator, Non-Profit Co-Founder and Executive Director of a county Chamber of Commerce.

I have had learning curves in some of the roles, even though onlookers might have believed that I entered each role with the total packaging and the business acumen needed to succeed. The truth is my relentless persistence to be a *lifelong learner* and my passion for creativity as I re-define myself and the world around me are tremendous driving forces that motivate me and give me the thrust to push me forward so that I can make positive strides in my gutsy leadership journey. I am wired to chase after excellence for myself and take others on the ride with me while I stay at the top of my game.

Stops

Not one of my business roles has come easy and without high costs of one kind or another. I'm just as human as the next person and have had to battle against issues with my health, business decisions and relationships. Aspirations to live a balanced life are not only noble, but I've learned that they are necessary. With the intense drive that is an attribute of gutsy leaders, I've had to build in what I call "Stops."

Stops force me to take a look at all the roles I play in life and allocate *quality time* to each. Balancing being a son, brother, father, grandfather, employer, entrepreneur, executive, CEO, uncle, cousin, friend, Christian, volunteer, coach, consultant, neighbor, co-worker, etc. is hard work, but extremely rewarding.

I have learned that imbalance in one role will cause imbalance in all the roles sooner or later. Do not fall into the trap of believing that if you chase and attain success at the cost of everything else, you will get an opportunity to make up for your failures in the other roles that you play. This type of strategy will only result in empty promises, disappointments and a life devoid of peace and joy. Your spouse, children, relatives, etc., cannot relive the lost years with you when you are ready to do so. Once those years and the opportunities of those years have passed, they are gone forever.

Gutsy Evolution

For me, I don't think I experienced a gutsy moment. I think I'm instinctively a transformational leader. So, I believe it is instinct that gives a leader the ability to pull from a reservoir of experiences. Instinct says, 'We've already got this. We know this.'

I've been through enough and tackled enough to know what to do. I think this can frustrate people around gutsy leaders because they're looking at the leader to go through the processes being executed to solve problems and asking if they can help. As a leader, you're pulling on experience as you execute so there's usually not a strict recipe that is being followed. I might say, 'I don't know what's next as of right now. I'm figuring that out as I move forward.'

I'm comfortable pursuing a path of uncertainty because I'm just the instrument being used to lead the team to solve a problem. I'm one hundred percent focused on the fact that I'm being divinely used to help solve a problem. The end result is a divine fingerprint on the solution. Most challenges faced by gutsy leaders are actually bigger than the leaders themselves, but most gutsy leaders are willing to go where others are not willing to go because they know they are just tools being used for a much larger divine purpose in the grand scheme of things.

Change Assignment — The Digital Disruption

I took on the herculean task of being named the Executive Director of the Monmouth County Chamber of Commerce. The chamber was founded in 1959 and has gone through many changes as the national business landscape has evolved.

The Internet and digital solutions have revolutionized all business models. Chambers of Commerce and their member businesses and organizations weren't exempt from what I call the *digital disruption.*

Many in business wish terms like Internet, websites, social media, search engine optimization, keyword marketing, new media, blogs, LinkedIn, Facebook, Twitter, G+, etc., never existed. I've been told by business owners that they dream of the day when they'll wake up from this horrible dream so they can experience business the way it was before the digital disruption. To those entrepreneurs I say, 'Dream on. We are never going back so either you adapt to the paradigm shift of the information super highway, or you become road kill!'

As the Executive Director of a county chamber, I have faced many challenges. Being brought in from a neighboring county in New Jersey meant that I had to become familiar with the people, culture, climate, practices and traditions of businesses in Monmouth County. I've discovered that every business area has its own DNA and leaders have to look at the pieces and study the DNA in order to get a deep understanding of the modus operandi of the area.

When I worked on Wall Street I had to do the same thing so I was able to tap into my memory bank for a previously used model to guide me through a new challenge. I knew it was time for a memory bank withdrawal.

Secondly, I had to develop a strategy for operating above the noise, drama and cliques. Change causes people who are resistant to change to act out. To them, anything that attacks the status quo is identified as *not good* and believed to be something that must be resisted and relentlessly attacked. The one thing that forces them to take a second look at change is the delivery of consistent, measurable and timely results. As a former accountant, I know the numbers will speak for themselves if the numbers are not manipulated. I've found it pays to shut up, step up, and let the numbers speak for themselves. This strategy has never failed me.

Another major challenge involved charting a digital course for the chamber in order to rebirth its relevance in the 21st century business community. Previously, one of the reasons businesses and organizations joined chambers was to legitimize their operation and serve notice to local communities about their credibility as reputable businesses. In today's digitally disrupted business environment, businesses and organizations look to chambers of commerce to assist them in *unpacking, understanding and utilizing* digital solutions that will help defend their market shares and impact their bottom lines.

Gone are the days when entrepreneurs joined chambers solely to be legitimized. Business owners now expect chambers to be members of their dream teams. Membership is now based on return on investment (ROI). They say, 'I'll pay my membership fee in exchange for you joining my dream team and assisting me in taking my business to the next level. The new relationship is now a partnership.

As executive director of a county chamber of commerce, I'm actually greasing the wheels of change and ushering in an updated mission for the 21st century version of a chamber of commerce. In this new hyper-competitive and evolving environment chambers find themselves thrust into, they have to answer the following membership question every day: 'What have you done for me lately?'

Change within organizations has become the one constant leaders can depend on. I thrive in this environment because I'm a change agent by nature. As a child I got into many *situations* because I always wanted to know 'Why?' Explaining to me that 'This is the way it's always been' even back then made my blood boil because I viewed the explanation as an excuse. My business tagline is *Excellence without Excuse*[SM] because I don't believe in forcing things to stay the way they are if current times call for something different. If you tell me something can't be done I need you to have the data to support what you're saying.

If not, the change-train will leave the station with you left standing on the platform wondering what happened.

A business associate of my wife once said, 'Many people are graduates of MSU, the University of Making Stuff Up.' As a leader I believe that since I've found that people you're leading will sometimes candidly give made-up reasons about why they can't do something. I say do the work and let the data identify your next move. My wife always tells leaders she coaches, 'Show me the data' because hands down, the data never lies!

Impatience

One challenge for me as a leader is my impatience. When I observe a problem that needs resolution my instinct kicks in and I go into execution mode, or what my family and staff call mission mode. The challenge with that is getting everyone else on the team in the same theater I'm in. Once I'm in mission mode I automatically go into an intense focus where my breathing and eye movement becomes sharp and calculated. Anything outside of solving the problem is a distraction.

People who want to spend time pontificating about the problem (MSU graduates) but not take steps to help solve the problem are generally the first people I remove from the problem-solving equation. Conversations about strategy are of the utmost importance and I get impatient waiting for other people to climb aboard the change-train. Over the course of my leadership journey I've discovered and used techniques to reduce my impatience, but it continues to be an area I have to consciously manage.

Disturbing the Apple Cart

Having instinct as my driving force allows change to come as a natural process to me. Change is actually something that jumpstarts me. I find that I always try to bring change to the conversation when it seems many other people try to avoid the topic. I constantly re-evaluate things to see how they can be made better and I bring change to the game plan.

Some say I'm a change agent who is focused on disturbing the apple cart since change is usually the first step for me. I'm not suggesting that I subscribe to the practice of changing things just for the sake of change. I believe that since growth is a by-product of change, as a leader I have to look at challenges through the lens of change.

Alone Time to Deal with Fears – Absorption Time

Carving out alone time helps me manage my own fears so I know how to remove and isolate myself so I can think and distinguish between what I feel and what the data tells me. I call this process my Absorption Time. I retreat so I can reboot, recalibrate and refocus. During those times I determine what my current weaknesses and strengths are, what the data tells me, how I can revamp things, how similar a new problem or challenge is to a previous one, and what it will take to solve the problem and move to the next level.

I study, research, analyze, challenge myself, and memorize the data. Then I work on marrying the data to my leadership style. When I re-enter the mainstream I'm more focused, determined and driven to lead people who are co-laboring with me.

I don't allow the people I'm leading to see the fearful side of me because I know they need to see my game face so they can confidently continue moving forward with me. This is sometimes perceived by others as me being stand-offish, but I know when I'm on the leadership stage everyone expects me to be ready to deliver at high levels. Taking time to be in solitude provides me with a safe space to get in touch with my inner self.

DNA Wiring

Humility guides me and I know it's not me by myself getting things done. True gutsy leaders acknowledge this and are generally the ones who won't turn around and say, 'Look at what I've done.' Gutsy leaders are forward thinking and are not distracted by the magnitude of challenges. Actually, the magnitude drives us even more.

We're risk takers and we have a boldness that people sometimes mistake for arrogance. We're cerebral because we're always thinking and almost can't turn off our minds. During periods of calm I play *what if* scenarios in my head. What if the overpass fell down onto the highway? What if someone walked in the restaurant I'm dining in and became violent? What if Google, Facebook, Twitter and G+ change their algorithms?

These what if games are where my brain actually searches for necessary and calculated moves that might be needed to attack unexpected challenges. I then store the scenarios in my memory bank so I can draw upon them when I'm tackling real-life challenges.

Execute Mode

A heightened awareness and myopic focus give me an adrenaline rush of excitement when I'm in execute mode. Something happens cerebrally and my levels of creativity and imagination are also heightened. My speech rate increases so I have to focus on slowing it down. I get pumped and ready to give a problem its walking papers because I believe I'm made for the giant leadership moment to tackle it.

Gutsy leaders are proficient so when we're in our leadership zones we can sometimes appear unfriendly and unapproachable to people. We're laser-focused to an extremely heightened degree and that can look intimidating when we're solving problems.

Once a challenge has been neutralized and solved,

many gutsy leaders like to fade into the background to get ready for the next challenge. Rarely will you see us hanging around to be interviewed about what we just accomplished. For a gutsy leader, solving the problem wasn't that big of a deal so they don't want to spend too much time sensationalizing it.

Why Us?

I'm convinced that we're all born for a specific purpose. For some of us the purpose is to lead. Part of the reality of that purpose is going through our daily life challenges. Somewhere in our gut we know we've been called to lead. Challenges prepare us to be able to operate from an instinctive and gutsy mindset. We know we've been made just for these moments.

Our experience banks get deposits with every challenge, although the challenges require withdrawals in order to solve problems. This is true if we've identified ourselves as leaders. We go through periods where we're summoned to use gutsy leadership in situations. Then, we experience periods where there's a steady level of awareness when we have to pull from our leadership experience banks. We actually go through a dry run in our minds about what can happen in different situations. The dry runs keep us comfortable with solving problems and challenges as they occur.

Final Thoughts

To each fellow gutsy leader or gutsy leader in development I say, 'Grab the bull by the horn and take your team members for the ride of their lives as you begin to build up your leadership experience reservoir or bank account. Go ahead, lead the train out of the station. That's the only way challenges will be met and solved!'

Leadership Mini Journal Entries

Over time I've developed the practice of writing leadership mini journal entries to capture and share transformational leadership lessons. I'm including some of these notes in this book to stimulate aspiring gutsy leaders who are wrestling with their leadership calling.

I call the notes journal entries because an accountant uses journal entries to balance the books. These leadership journal entries can be used to add balance to our gutsy leadership journeys.

COACH T. BIGGS II - JOURNAL ENTRIES

Move On

Everything happens for a reason, but sometimes the reason is simply that you made a bad judgment call. When this happens, RESIST throwing yourself a pity party, and immediately RECOVER, RE-DEFINE, RE-FOCUS, REBUILD, RE-DEPLOY and RE-ENGAGE. Don't allow a bad judgment call to derail the fulfillment of your life's purpose. (December 2013)

Go Full Throttle

Don't spend your whole life wondering, 'What if I had given everything?' When it comes to your life, don't settle, go full throttle. Be the difference that makes a difference. (December 2013)

Fear vs. Dreams

Fear is the assassinator of dreams. Being a dreamer is not enough. You have to be an overcomer of fear, through faith, in order for your dreams to survive the assassination attempts. (July 2013)

Laughter

Laughter is medicine. Self-medicate as much as needed. (October 2013)

No Drama!

Life's a journey, but you don't have to turn onto Drama Avenue. Don't sweat the small stuff. Do everything in your power to put distance between you and drama-filled folks in your life who suck you dry of joy, peace and happiness. (August 2013)

Success

'The road to success is always under construction.'
(Lily Tomlin)

Simple as 1-2-3

1) If your group is doing the same things you were all doing two years ago, then it's time for you to find another group.
2) If you are the smartest person in your group, it's also time to find another group. (January 2013)

Baby Steps

Baby steps are steps in the right direction and they are not to be despised because the summation of the steps is action leading in the direction of progress. I've seen so many people anesthetized by all the steps they have to take to complete a journey, but if you just focus on the first step, and then the second step, and so on, you will move closer to fulfillment because baby steps count. (December 2013)

Dream | Pursue | Ignore

People who jump to conclusions and speak without gathering all of the facts are the same people who may spend their entire lives trying to please. If you are ever going to pursue the passionate things in your life (your dreams) you have to be willing to ignore the drama-filled, fact-less, irritable, minutiae-focused individuals who insist on being in your space. In order to accomplish greatness, you have to be willing to ignore small-mindedness. Small business owners have to ignore so much in order to turn their dreams into reality. Don't miss the fulfillment of your dreams focusing on pleasing negative and non-supportive individuals. (November 2013)

Return on Time (ROT)

If you spend most of your time watching and reading garbage, after a while the smell of garbage will follow you and influence your thoughts and your behavior. You get twenty-four brand new hours every day. Invest them wisely in order to get a great return on your investment of time. Here's an example of what I call Comparative Return on Time (ROT):

1. You play online games on your computer daily for hours. As a result, you increase your proficiency on the game and move up to the level of expert. After a while you're playing additional games because you have developed a skill to play these games successfully. You do this for four years and at the

conclusion of the four years, you haven't acquired any marketable skills. Even though the games were enjoyable, the return on time invested was very low.

2. You decide your computer skills need improving, so you register for a four-year college program. Each day after work, you do homework and as a result you acquire marketable skills. You maintain your focus and sacrifice the time to get good grades. At the end of four years you've earned your degree, increased your skills, made yourself more marketable, and as a result you can now pursue opportunities that four years ago you didn't qualify for. Your return on time is very high.

The next four years are coming your way. You get to decide what your ROT will be. Choose wisely because you get to live with the consequences (good or bad) of your decision. (September 2013)

Opportunity

When opportunity knocks, please do not send 'I'm almost ready' to answer the door. 'I've been ready' will do a much better job. (August 2013)

Speed vs. Accuracy

When you substitute speed for accuracy you will end up at the wrong place early. (May 2013)

Necessary vs. Convenient and Popular

There are times when doing what is necessary trumps doing what is convenient or popular. It is during these times that the stuffing inside of you is tested. I'm being tested! (April 2013)

Preparation

Prepare during downtime so that you are ready when primetime comes! (March 2013)

Live Life Until You're Empty

I have experienced hatred and love. I have experienced heartache and joy. I have experienced poverty and wealth. I have experienced sadness and laughter. I have experienced sickness and wellness. I have experienced intolerance and tolerance. I have experienced discrimination and acceptance.

Each of these experiences have formed me to be the 'me' that I am today. I could not have become who I am today without each experience. Whether I was up or whether I was down, I have learned that there have always been three constants in my life in the midst of any experience I was going through. These three constants remind me and assure me that no matter what I am going through, I am not to be defined by the experience, but I'm to allow the experience to bring forth more 'me' out of me. My three constants have been God, family and friends. When you live a life that embraces each experience as a process that will bring forth the best 'you' out of you, you end up leaving this world empty of all that was poured into you. You committed to living your life in a manner that allowed all of you to come forth and be experienced by everyone around you. Leave earth empty of all that was poured into you. (February 2013)

Let Go and Be You

When you learn to be comfortable with yourself and be who you really are, you will begin to learn some amazing things about yourself and others. And to boot, it's liberating! Escape the prison of the 'pretend you' and give the world a glimpse of the 'real you.' There are way too many Xerox copy individuals out there, please don't deprive the world any longer of the real you. (January 2013)

Prison of Fear

To my fellow entrepreneurs:

If at first you don't succeed, what the heck, give it another try. Relentless pursuit in the face of adversity is necessary if you want to achieve greatness. Don't allow the prison of fear that others have voluntarily incarcerated their dreams in to deter you from your pursuit. There are costs to entrepreneurial pursuits, but in the end, they are well worth it. Remember that a dream deferred or delayed is not a dream denied. (January 2013)

CLARION CALL FOR GUTSY LEADERS!

Transformational leaders who lead from the front have to be prepared to take hits for decisions they make and for some decisions they had no part in making.

Gutsy leaders have to be strong enough to take bullets as they come so that the group being led is protected and can stay focused on accomplishing the mission.

One of the things that make this easier said than done is the reality that gutsy leadership can oftentimes be unpopular and lonely. Some people don't want to deal with that eight hundred pound gorilla in the room! We decided that this small footprint book would deal head on with that gorilla.

Gutsy transformational leadership requires a wherewithal and quick-wittedness that empowers a leader to say, *"We do not have time for a committee to discuss, analyze, re-discuss, and re-analyze this situation. There is a sense of urgency that we need to address now. The problem has been identified, and as the leader I will of course get input from the committee, but a decision has to be made before things get worse around here. I am charged to make the final decision and to take whatever hits come my way. I know there will be hits made by some of our Monday morning quarterback decision makers in or near the group. That comes with the turf. Now, let's go!"*

Not only might the committee (and possibly others) find that move to be unpopular, no one is going to want to stand next to, in front of, or behind the leader. Let's face it, in many instances no one else wants to take any bullets!

Gutsy transformational leaders do not enjoy taking bullets. Let's get that straight. We simply know that taking bullets comes along with the territory, and we have to be ready to take bullets before they're fired at us. That way we shield ourselves from at least some of the pain caused by the bullet, and we can control the amount of scarring from the bullet wound.

Leaders who lead from the front to transform communities will be lied about, talked about, laughed about, gossiped about and rumored about. Those are some of the bullets. Although those bullets might hurt for a while, gutsy leaders develop a system to perform self-triage so that they can continue leading effectively and persistently.

Gutsy leaders who lead from the front also recognize early on that they do not have the luxury of pausing to breathe while life happens. They have to take deep breaths while they remain laser-focused on moving people and goals forward. The leaders have to ensure that their leadership actions result in their voices surfacing in the conversations and actions of others.

In other words, while the gutsy leader is exhaling through whatever painful experience they might be going through, the depth of the message must still penetrate the hearts and minds of the people being led. That way, everyone continues to focus on moving forward and no one dwells on the possibility of the gutsy leader's fatigue. The leader's image is the first one that the universe sees, and the leader's voice is typically the first one that is heard. A picture of unwavering strength is required even though the leader might never receive a *thank you* for his or her efforts.

Some people might say that this is a suggestion for gutsy leaders to be inauthentic about his or her struggles. That's not at all the message here. Gutsy leaders do need to use extreme caution about making their personal exhaustion public because their persona is contagious. An exhausted, grumpy and malcontented leader can lead to exhausted, grumpy and malcontented followers.

Gutsy leaders do not wrap their minds around the words *can't, doubt, impossible,* etc. We do what we have to in order to get it done, and get it done well.

In this book, *The DNA of Gutsy Leaders*, you have read narratives from several gutsy leaders with different career paths and professions. These leaders partnered with committees and teams, but they knew that at the end of the day *their* signatures would be on the dotted line. The gutsy leaders positioned themselves at the front of the line and led their followers through challenging and unchartered experiences. *They seized their leadership moments. Now it's time to seize yours.*

21st Century Thief

The modern day thief of vision fulfillment is wasted time.
(T. Biggs II, December 2012)

ABOUT THE AUTHORS

Coach Terence H. Biggs II is Founder & CEO of Marketplace Dynamics, LLC, and is an entrepreneur who service marked the term, _Excellence without Excuse_^{SM}. Because of his results-driven digitally nomadic passion for disturbing the proverbial apple cart, the excuse – _it has not been done before_ – doesn't register in his psyche. His guiding business principles are honesty, integrity and fairness. With hands-on experience operating and leading several small businesses, Biggs approaches marketing and technology from the perspective of business owners. He interacts with clients in plain English versus in confusing tech talk. Biggs believes the Internet has its own set of complications. He provides easy-to-understand and hands-on Internet and Social Media professional development and training sessions. Biggs' experience includes that of Entrepreneur, Marketing Executive, Financial Executive, Business Founder, Sales' Executive, Philanthropist, Product Developer, Trade Delegation Executive, Former Retail Store Owner & Operator, Non-Profit Co-Founder, Board Member of the Jersey Shore Convention and Visitors Bureau, and Executive Director of a county Chamber of Commerce. His impressive business career of over thirty years spans throughout national and international borders and includes over fifteen years of experience as a Wall Street Financial Accounting Executive.

Dr. Sharon M. Biggs is an executive leadership coach, consultant, and trainer who for almost thirty years has filled the roles of Leadership Coach, Executive Director, Assistant to the Superintendent, Principal, Assistant Principal, and Teacher Leader. After having a corporate leadership career, her educational leadership work spanned from affluent, high-performing suburban and rural school districts to low-income, and state-controlled urban turnaround districts. She currently leads the Educational Leadership Development Team at Marketplace Dynamics, LLC (MD). Dr. Biggs is the author of four other books, all available on Amazon, including *The Silo Effect: Invisible Barriers That Can Destroy Organizational Teams*, a chapter book now in its second edition).

Email, Profile & Website Information:

Coach Terence H. Biggs II
CoachBiggs@MarketplaceDynamics.com
https://www.linkedin.com/in/terencebiggs
https://marketplacedynamics.com

Dr. Sharon M. Biggs
drbiggs@marketplacedynamics.com
https://www.linkedin.com/in/drsharonbiggs/
https://marketplacedynamics.com
Publications on Amazon, Barnes & Noble and CreateSpace

Contact the authors to schedule leadership team retreats, workshops, conferences, seminars and speaking engagements.